W9-AQM-285

ULITSA GERTSENA

18,20

INTERNATSIONALA

7

5

23

10

9

17,19

4

VOKZALNAYA

ULITSA

15

K L Y A Z M A

3

1. Statue of V. I. Lenin
2. Monument commemorating Vladimir's
   850th anniversary
3. Cathedral of the Assumption
4. Cathedral of St. Demetrius
5. Nativity Monastery
6. Assumption Cathedral of the
   Knyaginin Convent
7. Stoletov Museum
8. House in which N. Fedoseyev lived
9. Vladimir-Suzdal Architecture, History
   and Art Museum
10. History section of the Vladimir-Suzdal
    Museum

11. Industrial Production Exhibition
12. Exhibition Hall
13. Exhibition of cut-glass, lacquers and
    embroidery
14. Golden Gates
15. Former Gubernia Office Building
16. Shopping Arcade
17. Former Nobles' Assembly building
18. Statue of M. Frunze
19. Former boys' high school
20. Military Cemetery
21. Park of Vladimir's 850th Anniversary
22. Church of St. Nikita
23. Church of the Nativity of Our Lady

EX LIBRIS

FIRM VIGILANT ACTIVE

VINCIT AMOR PATRIÆ

THE REVEREND
Jasper Green Pennington

SERGEI GORDEYEV

VLADIMIR

A Guide

RADUGA PUBLISHERS
MOSCOW

Сергей Гордеев

Владимир

Путеводитель

(на английском языке)

Редакция литературы по спорту и туризму

Translated from the Russian by *Sheena Wakefield*
Editor of the Russian text *Marta Derzhavina*
Editor of the English text *Yuri Semyonov*
Assistant editor *Lyudmila Andrianova*
Designed by *Eteri Simonovich*
Art editor *Nina Scherbakova*
Maps by *Lyubov Cheltsova*

English translation © Raduga Publishers 1983

© Издательство ''Радуга'', Москва, 1983
English translation © Raduga Publishers 1983

Г $\frac{1905040100-299}{031(01)-83}$ 74–83

CONTENTS

PREFACE

'The dawn broke like a goblet of golden wine in which a ray of sunshine is entrapped. Silence hung over the vast, hushed world, with grey cottages in the foreground, the forest behind them, and the sunrise in the background. The forest lay in the hollow of the land, and through it, evidently, flowed a stream: only a stream could be the source of that gigantic zigzag of milky mist etched into the blackness of the forest. In the distance a cross on the dome of a church rose out of the mist.'

Vladimir Soloukhin, from

Vladimir Country Roads

Vladimir is one of the group of ancient towns in the east and north-east of Central Russia, which also includes Suzdal, Rostov Yaroslavsky, Pereslavl Zalessky, Yaroslavl, and Kostroma. These towns have in common their interesting history, the major role they played in the emergence of Rus and the Russian state, the great number of architectural monuments which have survived in them and are in a fine state of preservation, and the progress they have made in modern times. All these factors combine to make the area popular with tourists from abroad.

Vladimir is renowned for its 12th century white stone architecture: the Cathedral of the Assumption with its frescoes by Andrei Rublyov, the remains of the royal palace in Bogolyubovo, the Church of the Protecting Veil on the River Nerl with its incomparable proportions, the Cathedral of St. Demetrius with its wealth of stone carving, and the Golden Gates, a unique example of military building. These masterpieces remind us of the time when Vladimir was the capital of North-Eastern Rus, and stood at the crossroads of Russian history.

Other ages too have left their mark on Vladimir, in the form of restrained 16th century churches, 17th century buildings aspiring to grandeur; baroque and classical styles, and buildings representing the artistic experimentation of the turn of the century; in fact it contains all the architectural trends which have existed in Russia.

Vladimir is also distinguished by the use ancient architects made of its hilly terrain, especially the high bank of the River Klyazma. From its vantage point Vladimir looks out over the boundless distances beyond the river, as they disappear into the blue haze of the forests on the horizon.

Ancient monuments are under the protection of the Soviet government, and in Vladimir there is not one building of value which has not been restored.

Vladimir's museums also maintain direct links with the past. The local history museum traces the story of the town and surrounding area from ancient days to last century, when it was a small provincial town, the centre of its *gubernia*, then to Soviet times, reflecting the town's recent growth and the modern life it leads.

Vladimir is a unique town, and the impression it creates will depend on the observancy of the visitor, the length of time he or she spends there, the knowledge of the guide, and season and weather. Each season has its own charms in Vladimir: in late spring and early summer the first bright green appears, autumn brings its golden colours, and crisp winter days deck the trees, bushes, wires and fences with hoarfrost gleaming in the cold sunshine.

We hope that this guide will help visitors to find their way around Vladimir faster, understand the town's history, see its architecture, and also glimpse its modern life.

The eastern suburb of Bogolyubovo and the museum town of Suzdal, lying so close to Vladimir, are also part of the town's past. We include information on them in this guide, to provide a complete survey of the history and architecture of the area.

SOME BACKGROUND INFORMATION

Vladimir is situated in the centre of the Russian Plain of the RSFSR, 190 kilometres to the north-east of Moscow. It extends for 17 kilometres along the elevated left bank of the River Klyazma (a tributary of the Oka), intersected by deep gullies and valleys through which small rivers flow. The town covers almost 60 square kilometres, and has a population of 300,000. Its oldest part, where the ancient architecture stands, is situated on the high plateau between the Klyazma and the Lybed (which now flows underground), sloping gently down to the valley of the River Rpen (the Irpen in the past) in the east.

The Klyazma is 140–145 metres wide where it flows through Vladimir. When the snow melts in the spring the water level sometimes rises to six metres, and it has been remarked that at this time Vladimir resembles a coastal town.

Vladimir and the surrounding area have a continental climate. For five months of the year, from November to March, the average temperature is below zero, the coldest month being January (−11.4°C). Snow normally lies from late November to early April. The summer is quite hot, although rain is not unknown. The average temperature in July, the warmest month, is 18.1°C.

Long ago forest stretched right up to Vladimir. Now little natural vegetation survives in the town itself. Linden trees and poplars predominate, and maples and rowans are frequent. Larches have appeared recently, and birches are common in parks. Occasionally you come across trees not native to these parts, such as the blue spruce, horse chestnut and thuya. There are roughly 30 square metres of greenery per inhabitant.

The local bird population includes the sparrow, jackdaw, crow and pigeon. Swifts and swallows are common, as are chaffinches and starlings. In summertime seagulls soar over the Klyazma and the Rpen, while rooks build their nests in the tall trees in the old graveyard and the gullies. Tits and bullfinches are common in winter and much loved by the local residents.

Vladimir is the administrative centre for the region lying between the Volga and Oka rivers. It covers 29,000 square kilometres, with a population of one and a half million. The region has 21 towns and 35 large urban settlements.

Relief of the area is an undulating plain with heights ranging from 68 to 271 metres above sea level, traversed at roughly equal intervals by 150 small rivers. There are about 300 lakes, none of them large, most of them being less than two square kilometres in size.

As much as 40 per cent of the area's territory is covered by forest, with pines, birches, aspens and spruce. Oak, linden, ash and others, are rarer. The largest mammal is the elk; there are also spotted deer, wild goat, wild boar, wolves, Ussurian raccoons, and lynx. Fox, hare, squirrel, marten, stoat and beaver are also common species.

The region is poor in mineral resources. Limestone, peat, and fire and brick clays are of industrial importance, while there are natural sources of mineral waters. Mechanical engineering and metal working are the major industries, alongside the textile, chemical and glass industries. Vladimir Region is responsible for a sizeable proportion of the national output of excavators, electric motors, diesel locomotives, radios and record players, motorcycles, linen and cut-glass. The town of Gus-Khrustalny is a famous centre for glass and crystal.

Agriculture concentrates on beef and dairy production and potato cultivation. The main cereals grown are wheat, rye, oats, buckwheat and pulses. Vegetables are grown in suburban allotments, onions and cucumbers doing particularly well here.

Both a railway and highway link Vladimir and its region with Moscow.

HISTORY

Vladimir, like Moscow, is one of Russia's ancient towns; it is almost 900 years old. It has enjoyed times of prosperity and known periods of decline. This brief outline will concentrate on the most important periods in the town's past.

To understand Vladimir's place in Russian history, we must return to the Middle Ages. In the 9th to 13th centuries Kievan Rus, inhabited by the Slavonic tribes of Eastern Europe, with its capital the city of Kiev on the Dnieper, was one of the major powers of the time. The state extended from the Black Sea steppes in the south to the northern coast, from the Carpathians to the Oka and the Volga. The capitals of the apanage principalities included Polotsk on the Western Dvina, Galich on the Dniester, Chernigov on the Desna, a tributary on the left-hand side of the Dnieper, and Smolensk on the Dnieper, in the Russian heartland. To the north, on the River Volkhov, stood Novgorod, second in importance only to Kiev itself. Far to the north-east of Kiev, between the Oka and the Volga stretched a vast territory from ancient times inhabited by Slavonic tribes, the Krivichi and the Vyatichi, and Finnish tribes, the Meria, Muroma, Ves and Chud. The largest towns in this area were Rostov, Suzdal, Murom, Ryazan, and Yaroslavl. The land between the Volga and the Oka had certain advantages; the nomads from the south did not raid so far north, the rivers facilitated trade with the rich countries of the East, the forests and rivers provided food and furs in plenty, and fertile lands lay to the north of the Klyazma. These advantages caused farmers from the Slavonic tribes, their lands in the south of Kievan Rus destroyed by the nomads, to move up the area.

Rus maintained diplomatic and trading relations with Poland, Hungary, Bohemia and Sweden, and in addition traded with Byzantium, Germany, and Caucasian and Eastern states. Its resistance to the nomads not only ensured its own survival, but also contributed to the preservation of West European civilisation.

Crafts and trades flourished in unprecedented fashion in Kievan Rus, and it also saw the birth of literature, art and architecture of world importance.

This first state of Ancient Rus survived for over 300 years, although economic relations between various of its territories were unstable. The descendants of the Kievan princes, Vladimir I, Yaroslav the Wise, and Vladimir Monomakh, who inherited principalities, founded local dynasties which aimed for complete independence. By the mid-12th century Kievan Rus had disintegrated into several independent principalities.

At this time a new Russian centre of government and culture grew up on the north-eastern border of Rus in the area of Rostov and Suzdal. This was Vladimir. The recorded history of the town dates back to the 12th century, but it was founded much before that. Archaeologists have found evidence of a Meria settlement here in the first century A.D. The original inhabitants were later joined by Slavs from various parts of the Russian land. Their culture was more advanced than that of the local inhabitants, there were more of them, and eventually they assimilated the Meria. The Finno-Ugric tribes left their mark in non-Slav sounding place names: the Nerl, Kideksha, Suzdal, the Peksha, the Klyazma, and others.

The Rostov and Suzdal lands were part of the principality inherited by Vladimir Monomakh at the end of the 11th century. He conducted regular campaigns in the area to defend his patrimony from raids by other princes, and it was during one of these campaigns that Vladimir, named after its founder, was established as a town on the site of the ancient Meria settlement. The first mention of Vladimir in the chronicles dates back to 1108.

The local relief predetermined the size and shape of the new fortress. It stood on the high plateau bounded to the south by the steep bank of the Klyazma, to the north by the slope down to the Lybed, and to the west and east by gullies which were adapted into fosses. The fortifications ran for two and a half kilometres. In the first few decades of its existence the town had little or no political or economic influence. Monomakh's heir, Yuri Dolgoruky (the name means Yuri of the Long Arms, deriving from his habit of invading distant lands), already suzerain of the Rostov and Suzdal lands, had his heart set on conquering Kiev, and had little time for the fortress on the Klyazma.

Vladimir grew in strength with the ascendance of Yuri Dolgoruky's son, Andrei Bogolyubsky, who transformed the town into the political centre of Rus. When his father died in Kiev in 1157, Andrei Bogolyubsky renounced his legal rights to the Kievan Principality, making it apparent that its one-time epithet of great was no longer deserved. A little later, in 1169, Vladimir proved its superiority by force of arms: Andrei Bogolyubsky's forces captured Kiev. By establishing a new political centre Andrei aimed to halt the disintegration of the Russian lands.

Building began in Vladimir, which was to eclipse all other towns by its beauty. A tremendous amount of work was done over the seven years from 1158 to 1165. The town grew considerably in size, now occupying all the high plateau between the Klyazma and the Lybed. Its ramparts stretched for seven kilometres.

Monomakh's fortress was made the centre of the town. To the west of it lay the New Town with the triumphal Golden Gates. Not far from them stood the royal palace with the white stone Church of the Saviour.

To the east of Monomakh's fortress was the *posad*, the trading quarter, with its Silver Gates. There were several more gates in the town: the Copper Gates, Irina's Gates, Tradesmen's Gates, Ivan's Gates, and the Volga Gates, which led down to the landing stage on the Klyazma.

Vladimir resembled an elongated, undulating triangle, formed of three parts each surrounded by ramparts, with the main highway running through the centre. Just outside the city walls stood the Cathedral of the Assumption with its golden cupolas, which could be seen from a great distance all around.

The rule of Vsevolod III (1176–1212), who because of his numerous progeny was known as Vsevolod the Big Nest, was the time of Vladimir's greatest prosperity. Local architects and builders reconstructed the Cathedral of the Assumption after the fire of 1185, and then began work on the royal palace, which archaeologists have established was built of white stone and brick.

Vsevolod had twice had to put down rebellions (1176 and 1185) in the town. Aware that there might be further disturbances, he built his palace in the centre of Vladimir, next to the Archbishop's residence, unlike his predecessors, who had always resided outside the city. The royal and episcopal palaces were divided from the town by the stone wall of the kremlin. The marketplace was moved to the square in front of the kremlin, under the watchful eye of the royal guard.

Now all that remains of the palace is the Cathedral of St. Demetrius (1194–97), lavishly decorated with stone-cutting.

Vladimir revealed its beauty to travellers gradually, as they moved along the main highway from one part of the city, surrounded by earth ramparts, to another. But from a great distance, because of the terrain, the town could be seen in a single glance. It looked particularly lovely from beyond the Klyazma, bearing a slight resemblance to the view of Kiev over the Dnieper.

Local architects and builders had gained in experience during all the work that had been done, and while Andrei Bogolyubsky had still had to bring in builders from abroad, Vsevolod could use local men.

The 12th and 13th century architecture of Vladimir and Suzdal was of particular importance. Nowhere else in Rus was sculptural decoration, similar to traditional wood carving, so highly developed. The Vladimir icon-painters, trained in Constantinople, retained the Byzantine refinement, imbuing their works with greater warmth and humanity.

Wares produced by the craftsmen of Vladimir were renowned far and wide. In this respect Vladimir was second only to Kiev and Novgorod.

'. . . The people of Vladimir realised long ago that they could not make their living from the land alone, and so they left their villages to engage in seasonal trades. This is the origin of all those Vladimir icon-painters, bast-shoe makers, furriers, woolbeaters, felt-boot makers, saddlers, embroiderers, charcoal burners, tar-extractors, sickle makers, toy makers, basket makers, horn-players, bast-mat makers, tarrers, joiners, brush makers, wheel makers, trunk makers, coopers, carpenters, potters, brickfirers, copper-smiths, smiths, stone masons. . .' (Vladimir Soloukhin, *Vladimir Country Roads*)

The chronicles of Vladimir were of great literary importance, treating historical events in the context of Rus as a whole, in keeping with the ideas of the Vladimir princes, who aimed for political domination in Rus.

The descendants of the mighty Vsevolod were unable to maintain the unity of the Vladimir and Suzdal lands. Dissension arose between them, and as *The Lay of Igor's Host* put it, '. . . heads lie strewn like sheaves of corn, the threshers thresh with flails of steel. On that threshing-floor lives are laid down, the soul is winnowed from out of the body.' Vsevolod's strong state was now divided into several principalities, each ruled by individual members of the royal family. The weakening of the once great Vladimir and Suzdal Principality was to greatly influence the fate of Rus as a whole.

In 1238 Vladimir was overrun by Khan Batu's Mongol-Tartar hordes. They surrounded the city on the 3rd of February. Vladimir proved unable to resist a long siege. The best regiments had already perished in a battle near Kolomna, just to the south-east of Moscow. The prince had taken a small force and gone north to the forests beyond the Volga to raise a fresh host. The townsfolk were left to defend Vladimir themselves.

They repulsed Batu's first attack on the 6th of February. The following day the attack was renewed, the fortifications damaged, and the attackers poured in through the gaps. Most of the city's defenders lost their lives in the ensuing fierce street fighting. Batu put the city to the sword and the flame. The royal palace, the merchants' and craftsmen's homes were burned, and fire swept the Cathedral of the Assumption, where the royal family, Archbishop Mitrofan, many of the boyars, and the unarmed townsfolk had taken refuge.

After this first attack, Mongol-Tartar raids became a common occurrence, and each time the city was burned and pillaged.

The yoke of the Golden Horde greatly damaged Vladimir both economically and culturally: for a long time there was no stone construction, foreign trade ceased, and many crafts either declined or disappeared altogether. Despite all its troubles, a spirit of resistance and desire for new life remained alive in the city. In 1242 the people of Vladimir lent what assistance they could to Prince Alexander Nevsky from Novgorod in his fight against the Teutonic Knights. Later, Alexander Nevsky was Prince of Vladimir for ten years.

Vladimir continued to be thought of as the political and cultural centre of North-Eastern Rus. In 1299 the goal for which Andrei Bogo-lyubsky had strived in vain was attained: Vladimir became the seat of the Metropolitan, the head of the Russian Church. Thereafter until 1432, the princes of Vladimir and Moscow were crowned in the Cathedral of the Assumption.

In 1380 troops from Vladimir fought in the Battle of Kulikovo Field to free the Russian lands from the Golden Horde. Moscow, which had led the campaign against the Mongol-Tartar yoke, was recognised as the centre of the united Russian lands. Vladimir's importance gradually declined, but just as at one time Andrei Bogolyubsky had turned to Kievan art in building his capital, so the first Moscow princes turned to the cultural heritage of the Vladimir and Suzdal Principality. Moscow's stone architecture drew greatly on that of Vladimir. In 1395 the icon of the Virgin of Vladimir, the town's most holy relic, was ceremoniously moved to the Cathedral of the Assumption in Moscow. There was great respect in the new capital for ancient Vladimir. In 1408 Vasili I sent the best Russian artists with Andrei Rublyov and Daniil Chorny to repaint the Cathedral of the Assumption in Vladimir, after the city had been looted and burned by the hordes of Khan Edigai.

In the 13th and 14th centuries the city was subject to periodic raids and there was no expansion. Only at the end of the 15th century did craftsmen and soldiers move out into and settle new areas. The town had a very small population; even in the mid-17th century, when the raids had ceased, it was not above 1,000.

People earned their living by leather dressing, soap and candle making, and pottery. There were several distilleries, and tile production developed. From an inventory of 1684 we learn that the marketplace housed 392 stalls, and the Church of St. Paraskeva, the patron saint of trade. The wares sold were household goods, clothes, building materials, and foodstuffs.

The 17th century saw the revival of building in stone. The new edifices blended with the natural and existing architectural landscape. The 17th century churches, built in the Russian tradition, tend to be more complex in form, with greater freedom of composition, very ornamental and richly decorated with multi-coloured glazed ceramics. These features reflect the tastes of the new merchant class, which had grown in influence as a market developed throughout the Russian land. A plan of the town, drawn in 1715 by an unknown artist in iconic style, shows that it still retained its mediaeval appearance, with the log walls of the kremlin with 14 towers dating from 1491 to 1536, earth ramparts, the voivode's residence, a pond in case of siege or fire, and a maze of irregular streets lined with wooden houses.

In the 18th century most Russian cities experienced a kind of second birth, when the picturesque but decrepit, old, and disordered appearance of the town was replaced by strict, regular planning. Current ideas of state harmony and order dictated geometrical planning with a clearly delineated administrative centre, straight streets and wide squares.

Reconstruction work also began in Vladimir, which in 1778 had become the centre of the Vladimir administrative area, which later in 1796 became Vladimir Gubernia. On the whole the new planning worked, because it did not destroy Vladimir's topography or ancient architecture. The city therefore retained its individuality and attractiveness. There were, however, some not so happy choices, such as the bulky, parallelepipedal Administrative Offices (1785–90) between the Cathedrals of St. Demetrius and of the Assumption, which somewhat destroyed the harmony of the southern view of the town.

The 18th century did, however, see some of Vladimir's ancient architecture destroyed and spoiled. The town fortifications, no longer functional, were removed with governmental permission. As the town expanded the earth ramparts were removed in some areas, or in others adapted into orchards and vegetable plots. After the fire of 1778 the white stone churches of the Saviour and of St. George were demolished and replaced with new churches, and the Golden Gates were considerably altered.

Vladimir's rise as an administrative centre did little to promote its development. In the early 19th century it had two small textile mills, one manufacturing coarse, coloured cotton fabric, the other producing Flemish canvas, and duck for small sails. Of considerable importance were malt production and the dressing of high quality leather which was sent to St. Petersburg. Industrial establishments never survived long in Vladimir, however, one of the reasons for this being that the local authorities hampered their growth, fearing the concentration of large numbers of workers in the administrative centre.

Consequently an unusual situation arose, whereby Vladimir Gubernia was one of the most industrially developed regions in Russia, second only to the Moscow and St. Petersburg gubernias, while Vladimir itself had not a single large factory. The townsfolk continued to make their living by cultivating fruit and vegetables.

A grammar school and hospital were opened in the early 19th century, and a theatre in 1848. This, however, did little to change the general poverty of cultural life. Economic stagnation also affected the provision of the town with services. Most of the streets were unpaved and almost never cleaned, while the water, which had been piped since 1866, was not filtered.

1825 was the year of the Decembrist uprising by members of the nobility against autocracy and serfdom. Some famous Decembrists came from Vladimir, including Nikolai Basargin, Mikhail Mitkov, and poet Alexander Odoyevsky.

In the 19th century Vladimir served as a place of exile, and Alexander Herzen, revolutionary, writer, and philosopher, lived here in exile from 1838 to 1840 at 4, 3rd International St. (formerly Bolshaya Moskovskaya), near the Golden Gates.

Here Herzen was visited by his friends. He himself travelled illegally to Moscow to fetch his fiancée, from whom her relations were trying to part him. They were married in Vladimir. Herzen always remembered Vladimir with great warmth, and devoted a whole chapter, entitled 'Vladimir on the Klyazma', to the town in his book *Thoughts on My Past.*

Vladimir's population grew slowly but steadily throughout the 19th century. While in 1808 it had less than 6,000 inhabitants, by 1897 that figure was above 24,600. The town became more animated, and its people began to turn their attention to political affairs.

In 1892 the first Marxist circle in Vladimir was formed among the young people by Nikolai Fedoseyev, who arrived here on being released from prison in St. Petersburg. Despite police surveillance he managed to make contact with both young people with revolutionary ideas and with workers' circles in the gubernia's industrial centres. Fedoseyev, charged with producing and distributing among workers political leaflets was arrested and imprisoned in Vladimir. Lenin was aware of Fedoseyev's valuable work, and came to Vladimir in 1893 in order to meet him, but to no avail, because Fedoseyev's release from prison was postponed.

During the first Russian bourgeois-democratic revolution of 1905–07 strikes affected all the industrial centres of the gubernia. The textile-workers' strike in Ivanovo-Voznesensk (now Ivanovo, centre of the Ivanovo Region) was particularly stubborn and saw the establishment of one of the first Soviets in Russia. These were elected bodies in charge of the strike, which became the model for the later Soviet government. In Vladimir itself there were meetings and political protest marches, and railway workers and state department office staff went on strike.

The experience gained at this time and the subsequent preparatory work done by the Bolsheviks in the town facilitated a quick transfer of power to the Soviets of Workers', Peasants' and Soldiers' Deputies in October 1917.

We are reminded of Vladimir's revolutionary past by plaques on many houses where secret political meetings were held, underground printing presses operated and illegal literature was stored.

The Revolution brought social and economic changes to Vladimir almost immediately. At first the plan was to develop the textile industry, traditional in Vladimir Gubernia, but eventually mechanical engineering and the chemical industry became dominant.

In 1932 the Avtopribor Plant was built in the valley of the Rpen, on what was then the eastern edge of the town. It provided the first Soviet car factories with appliances. Now it produces approximately 450 items, including speedometers, windscreen wipers, gauges, manometers and indicator lights, supplied to factories both in the Soviet Union and abroad.

In the same year a chemical plastics factory (now the Vladimir Chemical Plant) opened next to Avtopribor. Its production includes various plastics, materials for heat and sound insulation and for manufacturing acetate silk, film reels, radio parts, kitchenware, toys, etc.

One quarter of Vladimir's inhabitants fought in the Great Patriotic War of 1941–1945. Women and adolescents manned the factories, producing what was necessary to defend the country. Ten hospitals were opened in the town, and approximately 40,000 litres of blood were donated for the wounded.

During the war a tractor plant was built, and in the spring of 1945 it sent its·first 500 tractors to the areas recently freed from occupation.

VLADIMIR TODAY

Vladimir today is very different from what it was before 1917. Then a town of officials, merchants, petty bourgeoisie and clergy, it is now a major industrial and cultural centre. Its fifty factories produce more than 2,000 items: tractors, electrical motors, precision tools, car appliances, furniture, pianos, clocks and watches, shoes, household and recreation goods. They export to 80 countries. The town was awarded the Order of the Red Banner of Labour in 1971 for the economic progress it had made.

Modern Vladimir is divided into several clearly delineated districts: the old centre, the new residential areas, industrial areas and the recreation zones both within and outside the town.

Dominating the centre with its narrow, shady streets rise the gilded cupolas of the cathedrals. The area is under state protection, and this ensures the survival of the architecture of value, and of those buildings which, although not of note in themselves, help to retain the original old atmosphere. These buildings have been renovated and adapted for use by organisations or as residential homes.

The protected area is surrounded on three sides by new, multi-storey buildings. The town is now 11 times larger than it was in 1917. It has three million square metres of residential space. Housing standards have also risen, with better planning and improved appearance both inside and out. Rents here, as throughout the country do not on average exceed five per cent of a family's income.

The town has now spread to the right bank of the Klyazma. There, among the natural woodlands, are a hospital serving the region, and a hotel. A trolleybus route along a tree-lined dike, links the main part of Vladimir with this park.

Both before and immediately after the Revolution there was almost no transport in the town apart from carts. Now over 100 trolleybuses, 60 buses and 250 taxis travel its streets every day.

The white stone railway station was built in 1976, with waiting rooms for up to 1,500 passengers, a hotel, restaurant and many other modern features. The station is approximately one kilometre from the town centre.

As in olden times, the Golden Gates are the main entrance into Vladimir

Statue of V. I. Lenin on Lenin Square   The Drama Theatre

The town has over 100 hospitals and clinics with a staff of 4,500 with higher and specialised secondary qualifications. Medical care is free of charge.

Sport is popular in Vladimir, and about 100,000 people are members of sports societies, which have the sports centre, stadiums, gymnasiums and indoor swimming pools at their disposal. Gymnast Nikolai Andrianov, national, European and world champion and Olympic gold-medallist, comes from Vladimir.

The town has over 50 ordinary secondary schools, specialised secondary schools and occupational training schools. There are also special music, sports and art schools, a Pioneer Palace and various children's clubs.

There are approximately 17,000 students, including some from Latin America and Africa, in the teachers' training and polytechnical colleges.

The first kindergarten opened in Vladimir in 1918, and now there are over 100 play schools and crèches.

The largest of Vladimir's scientific institutes is the All-Union Research Institute of Synthetic Resins (VNIISS), established in 1958. It works out new methods for the national chemical industry on the chemistry and technology of foamed plastics, ethers, cellulose and other types of heat-resistant polymers. The institute collaborates with scientists in the GDR, Poland, and Czechoslovakia on some questions. The Vladimir Research and Development Institute of Electromechanical Engineering develops new and improves existing designs of electrical motors.

A drama theatre opened in 1848. Here Alexander Lensky, the most renowned Russian actor of last century, made his debut, and the great Russian actress Maria Ermolova and Alexandra Yablochkina, People's

Artist of the USSR, performed. In 1971 it moved into its new building by the Golden Gates.

Vladimir has 140 libraries. The Gorky Library alone has roughly one and a half million volumes. The higher educational establishments, research institutes and the House of Political Education all have large book stocks. Books covering six centuries, from the 15th to the 20th centuries, are housed in the library of the Vladimir-Suzdal Museum. The total book stock of all the municipal libraries is over eight million volumes.

Vladimir has been the first step on the road to fame for many writers and artists. Nikolai Voronin (Dr. Hist.), famous for his studies of ancient Russian culture, began his career here in the local history museum. The newspapers of Vladimir were the first to print the works of Sergei Nikitin, the author of sincere and realistic short stories which capture the living Russian language. The area of Vladimir was to provide writer Vladimir Soloukhin with a major source for his books, which have now been translated into many languages. The Vladimir publishing house published Andrei Voznesensky's first collection of poems.

Professional writers, artists and architects currently live and work in Vladimir. About 15,000 local people are members of amateur art circles.

The people of Vladimir preserve all the best features of the past in laying new streets and parks. In 1977 the RSFSR State Prize was awarded to local architects, restorers, and museum staff for their work in restoring ancient monuments and opening museum exhibitions. Roughly two million Soviet and foreign tourists visit Vladimir each year.

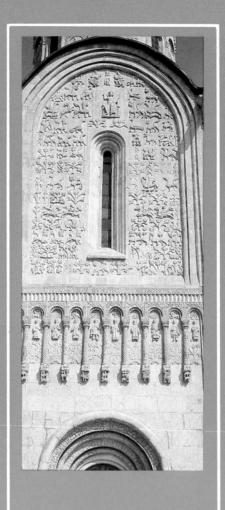

WHAT TO SEE
IN VLADIMIR

THE OLD TOWN

Visitors from abroad usually spend one or two days in Vladimir, which is enough to get a general impression of the town, see its important architecture, and visit two or three museums. Tours both by bus and on foot are on offer; the one we suggest is to be covered on foot, as the old centre is relatively small.

LIBERTY SQUARE

The town centre has always been the area between the Cathedrals of the Assumption and of St. Demetrius, now known as Liberty Square (Ploshchad Svobody), previously called Cathedral Square. In ancient times it was the market place. The square often saw the gathering of the home guard before a battle. In October 1917 the first Soviet decrees on peace and on land were read out here. Liberty Square is now the scene of celebrations and festive processions.

Vladimir celebrated its 850th anniversary in 1958, and to mark the occasion a monument sculpted by Dimitri Ryabichev and designed by Alexei Dushkin was

Monument in honour of the 850th anniversary of Vladimir

erected here on the site of the wooden Obelisk of Liberty which had stood there since just after the Revolution. The monument is in the shape of a three-segmented white stone obelisk decorated with relief sculptures standing on a granite base. The theme taken is that of the people as the maker of history, and is embodied in three bronze figures—a soldier, an architect and a worker. The former faces the Golden Gates in memory of the town's glorious past, the architect looks towards the Cathedrals of the Assumption and of St. Demetrius, and the worker holding a miniature tractor turns his head towards the town's new industrial districts. The relief sculptures are in the style of the carving on the old churches and echo the themes expressed in the bronze figures.

On the northern side of the square stand two mansions in Empire style, built at different times but sharing one long façade. The left corner building, built in 1826 by the Moscow architect Vasili Dregalov, housed the **Nobles' Assembly** (Dvoryanskoye Sobraniye). It is now the Army Officers' Club. The two-storey building with 12 Ionic columns and a relief frieze on the wall behind is interesting for the happy proportions given to it by the lengthened windows. The entrance hall is adorned with a colonnade and a wide staircase leads to the spacious rooms on the first floor.

In October 1905 a meeting was held in the building at which for the first time in Vladimir speeches against tsarism were made openly. Student Pavel Lebedev, who later became a well-known literary scholar, unfurled a red banner with the words 'Down with the Autocracy'. The authorities broke up the meeting, and Pavel Lebedev was cruelly beaten.

For a long time the hall on the first floor had the largest capacity of any in Vladimir. After the Revolution various conferences, meetings and congresses were held here; on the 25th of June, 1927 poet Vladimir Mayakovsky addressed the people of Vladimir here, reading a report entitled 'The Face of Left Literature', some of his own poems, and answering questions.

The right part of the ensemble was built separately in 1841 by architect Evgraf Petrov. Formerly it housed the boys' high school, and now refresher courses for teachers are held here. It is built in late neoclassical style, with a stately portico of Doric order. The semicircles above the windows contain models of lyres in stucco moulding. On the buildings is a plaque of grey granite bearing the names of former pupils who later became famous, such as writer Nikolai Zlatovratsky (1845–1911), artist Dmitri Kardovsky (1866–1943), author of some beautiful illustrations to Russian plays, Academician Anatoly Blagonravov (1894–1975), who did major research work on mechanical engineering and space exploration, and the poet Konstantin Balmont (1867–1942).

On the west side of the square stands a brick building in pseudo-Russian style, built in 1907 for the Town Duma (town council). Now it houses the Pioneer Palace. Earlier

The former Nobles' Assembly building

a two-storey wooden building with a gable roof stood here; the first floor housed the Duma and the ground floor the guard house. Next to it stood a sentry box, and morning and evening the guard was changed to the beating of drums and the strains of the national anthem.

THE CATHEDRAL OF THE ASSUMPTION

The Cathedral of the Assumption (Uspensky sobor) is the oldest of the buildings on the square; this magnificent architectural monument has shared the town's history since its founding. Andrei Bogolyubsky could not build a new political centre for all Rus without the support of the church; Kiev was then the seat of the Russian metropolitans and boasted the Cathedral of St. Sophia and the Pechersky Monastery with its relics of the first Russian saints, and Bogolyubsky had to ensure that Vladimir acquired the necessary religious authority: its own rites, sacred relics and beautiful churches in order to be able to compete with Kiev.

Work was therefore begun on the Cathedral of the Assumption at the same time as the town forti-

The Cathedral of the Assumption, view from the east

The ancient section of the Cathedral of the Assumption (the lower tier)

fications were erected. Bogolyubsky intended it to be on a par with the main cathedral of Kievan Rus, the Cathedral of St. Sophia, and he summoned builders from far and wide, including those skilled in work with white stone from the Romanesque West.

The foundation stone of the cathedral was laid on the 8th of April, 1158. The prince allocated the best villages and a tenth part of his livestock and income from trade to the cathedral, and consequently it was finished in three years' time. Soon its fame spread throughout Rus.

Standing in the most advantageous position on the high bank of the Klyazma, it dominated the town and surrounding low plain, its golden dome visible from afar.

From chronicles and more modern studies we know that originally the cathedral in plan was a slightly elongated rectangle with the semicircular triple apse on the eastern side. The façades also described the same figure, stood on end. The façades were divided by pilasters corresponding to the division internally into naves. The cathedral was surmounted by a dome on a drum with twelve windows.

In the semicircular *zakomary** gables were sculptures on the themes of three men in a burning fiery furnace, the forty martyrs of Sebastia, and the ascension of Alexander the Great. The belt of blind arcading around the centre of the façades was, with other decorative features, to become characteristic of Vladimir and Suzdal churches.

All chroniclers note the wealth of gold used on the building: the gilded dome, the open-work gilded tracery around the *zakomary* gables, above which were golden goblets and weather-vanes, and the gilded copper of the portals and the columns of the blind arcading.

Inside, the grandeur of the structure combined with rich and delicate decoration. Six cross-shaped pylons carried the high, painted vaults; the columns and pilasters of the walls were crowned by pairs of sculpted lions. An ancient chronicler wrote: 'Prince Andrei built a stone church of splendour in the name of Our Lady and decorated it richly with gold and silver . . . In the church he installed three gilt doors; he decked it with precious stones, pearls, and all manner of beautiful patterning; he illuminated it with gold and silver chandeliers, and the ambo he made of gold and of silver. There were many liturgical vessels, ripida and other utensils decorated with gold, precious stones and large pearls. There were three tabernacles made of pure gold and studded with precious stones. And the church was as worthy of admiration as the temple of Solomon . . .'

The most famous of all Russian icons, the *Virgin of Vladimir*, brought by Prince Andrei from Kiev, stood to the right of the Royal Gates in the sanctuary,

---

* Zakomara—In Russian architecture a semicircular or ogee arch type top of the outer wall of a building, duplicating the shape of the vault under it.

One of the cathedral's window bays, with traditional old Russian decorative painting

The fresco *The Procession of the Righteous to Heaven*, a fragment of the *Last Judgement* by Andrei Rublyov, the Cathedral of the Assumption, 1408

Interior of the Cathedral

which was separated from the rest of the church by rich hangings. The icon, a masterpiece of world painting, is now in the Tretyakov Gallery in Moscow.

A Byzantine artist depicts Mary, sorrowing over her son's bitter fate, as the child Christ clings to her. Her huge, dark eyes radiate love and tenderness, and a calm submission to her lot; they contain a silent reproach to the indifference of men, and the proud restraint with which she bears her grief. The icon soon became revered throughout Rus, and 200 years later was moved to Moscow, the new capital.

For 25 years the cathedral stood in all its glory as a religious and cultural centre. It housed an extensive library, and chronicles were compiled here. In 1185, however, Vladimir was ravaged by fire, in which, the Lavrentiev Chronicle tells us, 32 churches were burned, along with almost all the town. The cathedral did not escape the flames, and everything in it succumbed to them; the wooden struts burned out completely, and the white walls became black with soot.

The repairs undertaken by Vsevolod III involved major reconstruction which radically changed the cathedral's appearance. The old walls were boxed in by new ones, and four corner cupolas were added to the central one. Its wide façades were divided into five unequal sections, or *pryasla*. The three central sections corresponded to the original walls, and the outer ones were where the new galleries ran.

The sculpture of the three men in a burning fiery furnace was moved to the outer northern wall, and the gallery was built in part with the old stones with remnants of carving on them. The drums of all five cupolas repeat the blind arcading around the walls; above the arcading each drum has a cornice with a scalloped edge. The reconstruction work made the cathedral more spacious. Inside, wide arches were made in the old walls, creating an impression of airiness. The old interior, however, was preserved as far as possible, surrounded on three sides by the wide gallery formed by the new walls, from which you can see the blind arcading and part of the windows. The gallery, where the prince and his family and retainers stood during services, has remained unchanged.

The dark galleries were used as the royal burial chamber. Special niches in the walls contain the tombs of Andrei Bogolyubsky, the inheritor of his policies Vsevolod III, Prince Yuri Vsevolodovich who was killed in 1238 in battle with the Mongol-Tartars on the river Sit, other members of the royal house, and the writers of the Ancient Rus—Bishop Simon, one of the authors of the *Lives of the Fathers from the Pechersky Monastery in Kiev*, and Serapion of Vladimir, who vigorously opposed the feudal quarrels, and who saw the Mongol-Tartar domination of Rus as punishment for the moral decline and vices of society.

Hardly had fifty years passed since the first fire, when in 1238 the cathedral was pillaged and burned by Khan Batu. Only the scorched bare walls remained standing. The building was again looted in 1293, when even the copper flags on the floor were torn up. Not surprisingly, none of the works of art in the cathedral have come down to us, and so the simple and accurate accounts of the chronicles are doubly valuable.

Some important remnants of paintings from various ages have survived on the walls. In the blind arcading on the northern wall of the original church can be seen badly damaged figures of prophets with their scrolls and two peacocks on either side of the lower window. These are the earliest surviving fragments of Vladimir and Suzdal painting, and indicate that in the 12th century the whiteness of the outer walls was relieved by murals.

The frescoes inside were repainted during the reconstruction after the 1185 fire. Only one fragment can now be seen, showing saints Artemius and Abraham, on the western wall, to the left of the central entrance to the original building. The paintings give a frontal view of the figures, which are framed by painted arches. This form of enclosure was common at the time, and stressed the integral link of the wall-paintings with the architecture.

In 1408 new frescoes were painted by the outstanding artists of Ancient Rus Andrei Rublyov, Daniil Chorny, and others. Most of them have regrettably been lost; of the ones that survive the *Last Judgement* is in the best state of preservation.

In mediaeval times the end of the world was seen as being imminent, and the last judgement a reality, irreversible retribution for man's sins. Byzantine artists traditionally painted this scene on one vast flat surface.

Rublyov and his fellow painters broke with tradition by painting the scene on various walls under the gallery, blending the frescoes and architecture in such a way as to involve the viewer in the events depicted.

The arch beneath the gallery portrays angels with trumpets summoning the dead to judgement. On the vault, surrounded by six-winged seraphim, Christ is seated in majesty, while above him angels unroll the scroll of the heavens. Beside this fragment a medallion contains the beasts of the Apocalypse, the symbols of the four kingdoms: the gryphon of Macedonia, the winged dragon of Rome, the bear of Babylon, and the horned beast of the kingdom of the Antichrist. On the wall beneath the vault is the seat of judgement, on either side of which stand Adam and Eve, the Virgin Mary and John the Baptist praying for clemency for the human race. Here too are Peter and Paul, the elders of the apostles' tribunal on the slopes of the vault. On the northern pillar under the gallery we see an angel appearing to the prophet Daniel, and on the opposite pillar the faces of the righteous wives. Beside this pillar, above the arch, is an interesting but badly damaged painting of the earth and the sea surrendering their dead. The earth is depicted in the form of a woman with a staff in her right hand and a coffin in her left, and the sea as a woman with flowing hair, in her hand a sunken ship.

The concluding picture of the cycle is to be found in the southern nave. It shows the procession of the righteous with Paul at their head, to heaven (northern slope of the vault), the gates of paradise guarded by a cherub with a sword of fire, and the prudent thief (western wall of the nave), the Bosom of Abraham (the southern slope of the vault), and the Virgin and angels (the eastern wall of the nave).

Rublyov is also credited with the fragments of frescoes surviving on the pillar under the southeastern dome (the torso of a warrior) and in the sanctuary, as well as with decorative work on the arches.

Rublyov's treatment of the *Last Judgement* was innovatory; he mutes the ideas of punishment and retribution ever-present in Byzantine art, and a sense of gloom and tragedy are also absent. The spirit is one of optimism. The apostles who stand in judgement radiate kindness and sympathy, the faces of the saints and the righteous bear expressions of steadfastness and moral purity, while those of the angels show a dreamy serenity.

The scene of the procession of the righteous to heaven is painted expansively, in an epic style which echoes the idea that redemption awaits many people on Judgement Day. Rublyov is attracted by the beauty of the human body. The angels blowing their trumpets are particularly graceful, the suppleness and lightness of their bodies conveying the charm of youth.

The frescoes have unfortunately lost much of their rich colouring. Time has almost completely destroyed the light blue background, while the dark-red, velvety brown, rose pink and other shades have faded. Originally the colours gave the frescoes great force, and it was possible to divert one's attention from the subject and just admire the colours.

The elegiac softness of the painting, the exalted faces and grace of the figures, and the vivid colouring made the *Last Judgement* a celebration of mercy and justice.

The joyous nature of Rublyov's painting was in harmony with the spirit of the age, reflecting upsurge of national feeling among the Russian people after the Battle of Kulikovo Field in 1380, the turning point in Rus fight to liberate herself from the Mongol-Tartar oppression.

Opposite the cycle of the *Last Judgement* was the three-tiered iconostasis by the same artists, at the time the largest and most impressive in Rus. The biggest icons were in the Deisis row, with Christ in Majesty in the centre in light-coloured clothing, to whom were turned in prayer and homage the Virgin Mary, John the Baptist, archangels and apostles. The flat, three-metre-high figures, with slight differences in gesture and angle of the head, stood out against the golden background with their expressiveness and rich

The fresco by Andrei Rublyov on the southern arch, depicting heaven and forefathers

colouring: dark green with gold and dark-red, deep blue with maroon.

In 1773–74, when a new iconostasis in Moscow baroque style was built, the icons by Rublyov and his fellow painters were sold to the village of Vasilievskoye in Vladimir Gubernia, from where in 1922 they were sent to Moscow for restoration. They can now be seen in the Tretyakov Gallery and Leningrad's Russian Museum.

Despite the twists and turns of history, the cathedral's fame stood the test of time, and until 1432 the princes of Vladimir, and then of Moscow, were crowned here. For many years the Cathedral of the Assumption was considered a model of perfection and it was no mere chance that in the late 15th century the Italian architect Aristotile Fioravanti modelled his Cathedral of the Assumption in the Moscow Kremlin on the one in Vladimir.

After the Revolution the cathedral was placed under state protection, and restoration work began in July 1918. For five months a special commission of scholars, artists, restorers, architects and photographers studied the frescoes; and layers of whitewash and later oil and tempera painting were removed from Rublyov's frescoes.

Restoration and maintenance work have since been carried out at regular intervals. A heating and ventilation system has been installed, the deformed arches of Vsevolod's galleries have been strengthened, the cupolas and baroque iconostasis were recently gilded, and the frescoes secured.

The Cathedral of the Assumption is a functioning church.

In 1810, to the north of the cathedral, a new bell-tower with a tall gilt spire was built on the site of the old tent-shaped one, which had been struck by lightning.

Although somewhat eclectic, it has become an integral part of the town's architecture, and its main high point. Lancet arches were constructed in the lower tier, so that the view of the cathedral might not be obscured. In 1862, however, the **Side-chapel of St. George** was built between it and the bell-tower, and the arches, their original purpose now defunct, were filled in.

Between the Cathedrals of the Assumption and of St. Demetrius stands the long, three-storey building of the Gubernia Administrative Offices, built in 1785–90 in the Russian neoclassical style. The building has an austere, ceremonial appearance. The protruding central and side sections on the front façade on the first- and second-storey levels have semi-columns and pilasters of Corinthian order.

The offices housed Vladimir's first printing-press, established in 1797 by the Moscow publisher Mikhail Ponomarev. During his exile in Vladimir Alexander Herzen worked here in 1838–40 as the editor of the unofficial section of the *Vladimir Gubernia News*. He initiated the publication of articles on the economy, history and ethnography of Vladimir Gubernia,

The Cathedral of St. Demetrius

which were important in promoting local studies.

The first storey of the building housed the district court, which was the scene of some important trials in the late 19th and early 20th centuries. In May of 1886 the court heard the case of the Orekhovo-Zuevo workers who had been involved in the 1885 strike at Morozov's factory. The accounts of the accused and the witnesses made it apparent that the situation at the factory was extremely un-savoury, and the strikers were ac-quitted. After the strike the gov-ernment was compelled to pass a law putting a ceiling on fines in factories.

The square in front of the offices was untended until the end of the 19th century, and here soldiers were drilled, or Caucasian horse-men or tight-rope walkers per-formed. In 1902 a park was laid out here, becoming known as *Lipki* (Lime Trees) *Park*.

Carved decorations on the south façade of the Cathedral of St. Demetrius

THE CATHEDRAL
OF ST. DEMETRIUS

In August and September 1941, when the Nazi army was advancing on Moscow leaving towns and villages ruined and burning in its wake, the restorers in Vladimir were at work repairing the Cathedral of St. Demetrius (Dmitrievsky sobor). It was in danger of collapsing: the main arches had sunk and developed cracks, one of the pillars supporting the dome had slipped, and the walls too had large cracks. The church was in need of major and expensive repair work, which could only be done, and was done, after the war. In the meantime measures had to be taken urgently to prevent the cathedral from collapsing. Vladimir architect Alexander Stoletov's plan to insert a concrete steel band around the entire perimeter of the wall and place strong metal braces along the axes of the pylons to counteract the thrust force was adopted.

It is only thanks to these measures, taken when they were, at what seemed to some an inappropriate time, that the cathedral still stands where it has stood for almost eight centuries. On this spot, the highest in Vladimir, it stands, overlooking the Klyazma, meadows and forests.

The Cathedral of St. Demetrius was built by Russian craftsmen in 1194–97 as the royal church of Grand Prince Vsevolod III, and dedicated to the prince's patron saint, St. Demetrius of Salonica (Vsevolod was named Dmitri at his christening). Its splendour was intended to enhance the fame and power of Vladimir's ruler.

Originally the cathedral was surrounded by other palace buildings, and a series of passageways connected them with it. It had covered galleries on three sides, and the northern and southern fronts had towers with stairs leading to the royal galleries.

The cathedral shared the same sad fate as many of Vladimir's ancient buildings. It suffered from fire, was looted, and its original shape was altered.

It was built when Vladimir and Suzdal architecture was already in its fifth decade, having progressed from the severe, bare buildings of Yuri Dolgoruky's time to the elegant, decorative churches of Andrei Bogolyubsky with their intricate carvings. This was the age when architecture reflected royal splendour and might.

The cathedral is remarkable for its clean outline. The white stone façades are divided into three by elegant pilasters, each section culminating in a *zakomara* gable. There is a richly ornamented portal in each façade. Above the vaults rises the golden helmet of the cupola crowned with an openwork cross and half-moon, and a weathervane in the form of a dove made of sheets of copper. The half-moon was the symbol of one of the ancient mythological goddesses, and its position under the cross would seem to symbolise Christianity's triumph over paganism.

The cathedral with its monumental character is an echo of the age in which it was built, for this was the Vladimir-Suzdal Principality's most prosperous period. When the author of *The Lay of Igor's Host* calls on the Russian princes to defend their native land, he reminds them of the might of Prince Vsevolod of Vladimir who could '. . . splash away the Volga with his oars, scoop up the Don with his warriors' helmets.'

The rich carving on the walls includes both religious themes and pagan motifs.

The right-hand window on the south front is surmounted by a sculpture of the ascension of Alexander the Great, symbolising the divine origins of royal power. Vsevolod himself is portrayed, surrounded by his genuflected sons, above the left-hand window of the northern wall.

The west façade has sculptures of the labours of Hercules, his combat with the Nemean Lion, the Stymphalian birds and the Hydra of Lerna, which in the hands of the Vladimir sculptors became a huge bird.

The central arch of all three fronts repeats the same theme of David the Harpist, who in mediaeval art was linked with the theme of the celebration of the beauty of the world.

The sculptures at the level of the blind arcading are devoted to those who sacrificed themselves for the Christian faith. Most of the original figures were eventually replaced with new ones, but some of the sculptures on the west front, and all of them on the right side of the north façade have survived. They include the first Russian saints Boris and Gleb, who were very revered at the time. They were killed in 1015 by their elder brother in an internecine struggle.

Much literature has been written on the carvings on the Cathedral of St. Demetrius, from the time of the first studies over 100 years ago, to Georgi Wagner's authoritative work *Sculpture in Ancient Rus*. Wagner wrote that behind the sculptures on the cathedral lies a kind of a general idea which combined Vsevolod's political aspirations, and the ideas held by the Russian people on the importance of strong rulers, the complex structure of the world, its magnificence and beauty, and the struggle of conflicting forces within it. Secular mingled with religious, canonical with apocryphal, and feudal with folk.

Many attempts have been made to establish the origins of the animal and bird motifs, which include lions, centaurs, panthers and fantastic birds. Assyria, India, Alexandria, Asia Minor, Byzantium, Saxony, Swabia, Northern Italy, Galich, the Caucasus and the Balkans have all been considered as possible sources. In fact, animal and bird motifs were common in folk art throughout the mediaeval world, and while the Vladimir artists were undoubtedly influenced by the art of neighbouring countries, they created something uniquely their own. Austrian scholar F. Halle in her book on Vladimir and Suzdal sculpture noted that the carvings created such an original and complete picture that all the eastern and western elements could not be called either Asian, Byzantine, or West European, but only specially Russian.

Of the original wall-paintings inside only fragments of the *Last Judgement* on the central and southern naves under the galleries have survived. The other frescoes, damaged in the 1238 and 1536 fires, were painted over in oil in the 18th century, and later removed altogether.

Immediately after the Revolution the cathedral was placed under state protection as being of extreme importance, and restoration work was begun under Igor Grabar, renowned Soviet artist and art historian. Inscriptions, and whitewash and cement layers were removed from the frescoes which were secured and attributed. The most recent restoration work was undertaken in 1968–70 by a team from the Vladimir restoration workshop under Alexander Nekrasov. On completion of the work the frescoes were photographed and published.

Stylistic features lead us to believe that the frescoes were done by a group of painters under the guidance of a talented and experienced Byzantine artist, possibly from Salonica. It is assumed that to him belongs the total conception of the cycle, and that he himself painted the twelve apostles and the angels on the southern slope of the central vault. The paintings are in perfect classical style, the figures of the apostles being purely Greek, with the expressive features of the Greek school of portraiture, shown in unconstrained attitudes. Note the virtuosity and variety with which the raiment is done. The artist is equally at ease with the finest of gradations in tone, achieved by gradually lightening a darker tone with very liquid paint, and rich highlights placed with bold strokes. The light semitones create a soft, rather cold range of colour, through which a golden light seems to radiate from the centre.

The figures of the angels on the northern slope of the central vault are in a completely different style. The manner is less confident, the faces lack ideal grace; instead they are realistic, and painted with greater intimacy. The righteous wives on the south nave are given Slavonic features and dressed in Russian attire. The artist's penchant for patterned and decorative depiction of the vegetation in the Garden of Eden indicates his Russian origin, and he was probably from Vladimir itself.

By the western wall, to the right of the entrance, is a marble statue from London over the grave of Count Roman Vorontsov, the first governor of Vladimir Gubernia, who died in 1783.

The cathedral houses an exhibition on its history and restoration.

Beside the cathedral stands a round hummock formed by the soil removed to make way for the foundations of the Administrative Offices. The view of the Klyazma valley from here is marred only by the railway line, which was unhappily laid along the river in 1861.

THE NATIVITY MONASTERY

To the east of the Cathedral of St. Demetrius an 18th century whitewashed brick wall with towers and ornamental loop-holes runs along the ridge of the ramparts, following their smooth curve. There is a particularly fine view of the wall from the Vladimir Hotel and the railway station. This is the wall of the Nativity (Rozhdestvensky) Monastery.

Founded in 1191, it soon became renowned throughout Rus, and was the most important monastery until 1561, when precedence was ceded to the Monastery of the Trinity and St. Sergius (Troitse-Sergiyevskaya Lavra) in Zagorsk near Moscow. From the late 13th century until 1328 the monastery was the seat of the head of the Russian Church. Rich gifts were made by the senior clergy and other major figures, such as tsars Ivan the Terrible, Fyodor Ioannovich, and Boris Godunov, Patriarch Adrian, Prince Ivan Shuisky, former Tsarina Evdokia Lopukhina, a prisoner of the convent of the Protecting Veil in Suzdal, and Prince Alexander Menshikov. By the beginning of the 18th century the monastery owned approximately 8,000 serfs, farming lands and fisheries, a mill on the Nerl, and the Suzdal *podvorie* (coaching inn) in Moscow.

In 1744 Empress Elizaveta Petrovna ordered the cloisters to be abolished, and the higher orders of the clergy established their residence here.

The monastery played a major role in the history of Russian chronicles. It has been suggested that the chronicle code of 1305 was kept here; it was from this that the copy which became known as the Lavrentiev Chronicle was made. The manuscript copies of the Voskresenskaya Chronicle and the *Gradual Psalms* were kept here, brought in the 16th century by the monastery's Archimandrite, Iona Dumin. Here too lived Father Superior Simon, politician and writer of the early Rus.

The oldest building in the monastery was the **Church of the Nativity of Our Lady** (Rozhdestva Bogoroditsy) erected during 1192–96. Its shape was similar to that of the Cathedral of St. Demetrius, but more austere. Only the arches of the portals and the capitals had white stone carving, and instead of the splendid blind arcading typical of Vladimir churches of that time, a modest belt of dog-toothed triangles encircled the walls.

The outstanding state and military leader Alexander Nevsky was buried here on the 23rd of November, 1263. He died in Gorodets on the Volga as he was returning from a diplomatic mission to the Golden Horde to avert a fresh punitive raid to the Vladimir area as a reprisal for the revolt of the town's poor folk against the tribute collectors. In 1724 Peter I, thinking of Alexander Nevsky as his forerunner in the fight for national independence, had his remains transferred to St. Petersburg.

In the mid-19th century the dilapidated church was dismantled and then rebuilt in an exact copy of the original. Next to it stood a 17th century octagonal tent-roofed bell-tower. Both these buildings have unfortunately been lost.

All the surviving buildings date from the 18th century. The most important is the archbishop's residence in restrained baroque style. In the late 19th century it housed the archives of the Alexander Nevsky Fraternity, which consisted of a collection of old icons, vestments, utensils, documents, 15th to 18th century manuscripts and old editions of books. Most of the collection is now the property of the Vladimir History Museum. The residence included the 17th century Holy Gates, now hidden by later buildings.

THE STOLETOV MUSEUM

Walking round the monastery walls, we come out onto 3rd International St. (ulitsa Tretiego Internatsionala). The corner house, No. 59, is the **Stoletov Museum**. It once belonged to the Stoletov merchant family, from which came the brothers Alexander and Nikolai Stoletov, the great physicist and the famous general. The museum was opened in 1976 in the wooden wing, looking out onto the 12th century ramparts.

The house has been restored, and the current lay-out is the original one. In the first room hang 19th century engravings of Vladimir and photographs, one of which shows the boys' high school, which both Nikolai and Alexander finished with honours. Here too is a manuscript of a magazine, one of whose authors was Alexander, and pages from his diary which recreate the atmosphere of the Stoletov household.

The salon has been restored to its original appearance of 1860s and 1870s, based on Alexander's diary, drawings, and the recollections of friends and relatives. The comfortable furniture, old piano, the dark wallpaper and portiere, the wall-clock, the mirror stretching the full height of the room, the chandelier, and the photographs in their ornate and oval frames recreate the impressions of the measured and somewhat patriarchal life of a merchant family. Many of the objects actually belonged to the Stoletovs: the barometer, the Réaumur thermometer to the right of the entrance door, the needlework basket, photograph album, the crockery in the cabinet, and the dining table with its table-cloth. The portrait in the large oval frame is of Grigory Stoletov, the head of the family, and next to it hangs a photograph of his wife Alexandra.

The room leading off the salon covers the life of **General Niko-lai Stoletov** (1834–1912). His military career began in 1854 immediately after he graduated from Moscow University, when he volunteered for the army during the Crimean War of 1853–56. The St. George's Cross displayed here was awarded to Nikolai for his exceptional courage in the battles at Inkerman. At that time he was offered his first commission and became an ensign. After the war he graduated from the Academy of the General Staff, and served in the Caucasus and Turkestan. In 1869, as commander of a military detach-ment, he founded the town of Krasnovodsk, now a port on the Caspian Sea. He became famous during the Russo-Turkish War of 1877–78, when he led the Bulgari-an Home Guards, which he helped to recruit, and which fought with the Russian forces in the Balkans. Some of the exhibits here, includ-ing weapons from that period and the uniform of the Home Guards, were donated by Bulgarian mu-seums. Nikolai Stoletov himself helped to design the uniform, which combined traditional Bul-garian features with suitability for the climate.

Nikolai Stoletov was also a geographer, and displayed are some of the instruments he used when in charge of the 1874 expe-dition to study the Amu Darya (Oxus) basin in Central Asia. The expedition conducted a topo-graphical survey, and studied the climate, history and ethnography of the area. The Russian Geo-graphic Society awarded Nikolai Stoletov a gold medal for this work.

The next room is devoted to the life of **Alexander Stoletov** (1839–96), professor of physics at Moscow University, and the found-er and leader of the Russian school of physics. His particular field was that of electricity and magnetics and he was made famous by his study of the photoeffect, the abili-ty of light to create electric current. The photocell he invented was later to be widely used in automatic instruments, telemechanics, photo-metry, the cinema, optics, and astrophysics. Solar batteries on rockets and satellites function on the basis of the photoeffect.

The exhibition includes all the editions of Stoletov's works pub-lished in his lifetime, his manu-scripts, the works of his pupils and followers, and letters to him from the most important scientists of the time.

One of the photographs shows a view of Heidelberg, where, after graduating from Moscow Univer-sity, Alexander Stoletov attended lectures by the prominent phys-icists Hermann Helmholtz, and Gustav Kirchhoff, and learned how to conduct experimental work. There is also a photograph of the outwardly unremarkable building which housed the physics laborat-

The Stoletov Museum

ory of Moscow University founded by Alexander Stoletov in 1874, and the first in Russia. Of particular value are the apparatus from this laboratory, donated by Moscow University, including the apparatus Stoletov himself devised for investigating the photoeffect.

Here too is Alexander Stoletov's badge from the international electrical exhibition held in Paris in 1881 to coincide with a congress on electricity, at which Stoletov represented Russian science.

Alexander Stoletov is a classic example of a scientist who was both a major researcher and a brilliant teacher; over 30 years he trained many talented physicists. The exhibition has copies of the textbooks he wrote, including his remarkable *Introduction to Acoustics and Optics*, students' papers with his comments, and other material. Also here is his only award, the French Légion d'Honneur, recognition of his services

to world science. In his own country the doors of the Academy of Sciences were closed to him because of his directness, refusal to curry favour, and his defence of scientific truth.

The walls of the small salon are lined with the portraits of the Stoletovs' friends. Alexander maintained a lifelong friendship with his student Nikolai Zhukovsky, whom Lenin named as the father of Russian aviation. Alexander's love of music drew him to the composer Sergei Taneyev, also from Vladimir. Another friend of the Stoletovs was the composer's brother Vladimir Taneyev, a sociologist and barrister, whom Karl Marx in a letter to the Russian historian Maxim Kovalevsky described as a loyal friend of freedom for the people.

The bookcase here contains what remains of the Stoletovs' library. Alexander left his scientific collection to Moscow University, where it is still kept.

The final room records how the memory of the Stoletovs is today revered. Alexander's death coincided with the coronation of Nicholas II, the last Russian Emperor, and no official mention was made of Russian science's great loss. Alexander's friends and fellow scientists alone paid tribute to him. Only in Soviet times his services were recognised. The display includes his collected works, published after 1917, and books about Stoletov. There is a copy of the statue of Stoletov by the sculptor Sergei Selikhanov, erected in front of Moscow University. Streets in Moscow, Vladimir and Novosibirsk have been named after him.

Two show-cases display items sent from Bulgaria: they are the medals with which Nikolai Stoletov was decorated, plates of the streets named after him in Pleven and Gabrovo, gifts to Vladimir from the Bulgarian village of Stoletovo, and the handful of earth sent to Nikolai Stoletov's grave with this note to the people of Vladimir: 'Friends! This is a handful of Bulgarian earth for which your General Stoletov fought.'

THE VLADIMIR-SUZDAL ARCHITECTURE, HISTORY AND ART MUSEUM

The Vladimir museum was founded in 1854 on the initiative of regional historian Konstantin Tikhonravov. The two-storey building in pseudo-Russian style at 64, 3rd International St. was built specially for the museum in 1903 by architect Pyotr Begen. Various decorative elements from ancient Russian architecture are used on the façades. Profiled brickwork features on the belt between stories, the cornice, and the *nalichniki*, the decorations around the window frames. Coloured tiles are set in the niches of the cornice, the corner blades and the piers between the windows on the first floor. The entrance is through a porch typical of Russian wooden architecture.

In 1958 the Vladimir museum was amalgamated with the one in Suzdal, and in 1974, for the first time in the Soviet Union, a complex of all ten regional studies, art and memorial museums in the area was formed on the basis of the Vladimir-Suzdal Museum, with one single stock of exhibits and a common style of display.

The museum is a research and educational body; its property consists of 320,000 architectural, historical and other items. Of particular value are its collections of archaeological finds, coins, pottery, weapons, fabrics, manuscripts and old editions of books, cut-glass, lacquered miniatures, and paintings by Russian and contemporary Vladimir artists. It is famous for its collection of icons.

The museum has a reference library of over 50,000 volumes on history, art, regional studies, material culture, and the natural sciences.

The museum is visited annually by roughly two million people, and over 22,000 guided tours are given in Russian and the main European languages.

The building on 3rd International St. now houses a permanent exhibition on the history of the Vladimir region. The first rooms deal with prehistoric times, and contain unique finds from excavations on the site of the Paleolithic settlement of Sungir (see p. 86). There are a few exhibits from the next, the Mesolithic era (10th to 5th millennia B.C.), a time when man began to venture into unexplored areas. Among them are work tools common to previous ages, and flint-tipped arrows. The invention of the bow and arrow was a major turning-point in the development of the primitive tribal communities based on hunting and fishing.

The Neolithic era, the New Stone Age, (5th to 3rd millennia B.C.), is marked by improvements in implements, their variety and adaptation to specific purposes. The exhibits include clay vessels with a round bottom, usually decorated with some kind of pattern. Vessels from the area between the Volga and the Oka are character-

In the Stoletov house-museum

ised by an alternating pattern of hollows and ridges.

Next we come to the Bronze Age. The second millennium B.C. saw the appearance in the area of tribes belonging to the Fatianovo culture, the name taken from that of the village near Yaroslavl on the Volga, where a burial site was discovered. Metal was coming into use, and the display includes bronze axes, knives and spear tips. Bronze, however, was a rare commodity, and had to be brought from afar, and so most of the items are of stone. Advanced methods of treating it had developed, and the axes here are the best polished stone implements found on the territory of the Soviet Union.

Many iron domestic utensils and ornaments have survived from the Finno-Ugric tribes of the 6th to 10th centuries, and from the Slavs who arrived in the area in the 10th century A.D.

The section on the Vladimir-Suzdal Principality is particularly well-stocked. As the exhibits show, agriculture and fishing were the main forms of livelihood; many and varied were the goods produced by the local craftsmen: smiths, armourers, jewellers, bone carvers, glass-blowers, potters, and others. Many of them are of extremely high quality.

The large model in the centre of the room recreates the Vladimir of those days. Displayed are well preserved oak logs from the fortifications, and carved stones which were once part of the Cathedral of the Assumption and other churches.

Now on display, after many years of complicated restoration work, is the unique icon of the *Bogolyubovo Virgin*, pre-dating the Mongol-Tartar invasion. It was commissioned in the 12th century by Prince Andrei for the Cathedral of the Nativity in his residence outside the town, and it played a major role in his political aspirations. The Virgin is depicted full-length, appealing to Christ. It is in the best Byzantine traditions, a portrait of psychological depth. The colours are soft, with many gradations of tone.

There are many excellent original works also in the rooms dealing with the region as part of the centralised Russian state, such as painted tiles, secret locks and jewellery from the boyar and merchant circles. There are rich gifts from princes and boyars to cathedrals and monasteries: embroidery with pearls, silver articles, and books in expensive bindings. Attention is always attracted by the "lean" 17th century candle from the Church of Our Lady in Vladimir. This is a tall (116 cm) candlestick in the shape of a hollow wax cylinder with bright decorations in three colours. The upper half has a belt of decorative inscription, which includes the names of the Vladimir merchants who donated money for the building of the church.

The 15th century icon of St. Nicholas with scenes from his life is particularly valuable. It was discovered under six layers of overpainting by restorers. Another work shown here is the icon of the *Vladimir Virgin* from the 15th century, attributed to Andrei Rublyov.

Textile mills began to appear in the area in the time of Peter I. An ordinary piece of printed fabric is interesting as an early example of factory-produced linen. The clothing and furniture displayed reflect changes in the everyday life of the ruling classes. The end of the 17th century saw the beginning of secular portraiture, done in the iconic manner. Examples are the portraits of Tsarina Natalia Kirillovna and Tsarevich Alexei. The icon of *The Flood* from the late 17th century is an early predecessor of Russian sea-scapes.

The first floor covers the history of the area from the late 18th century. Above the map of Vladimir Gubernia, formed in 1792, are the coats of arms of Vladimir itself and the towns which were the centres of the uyezds comprising the gubernia. The central figure in Vladimir's coat of arms is a lion, as it had been from the 12th century. The lion had been the royal symbol of the Vladimir princes from the time of Andrei Bogolyubsky. The shield of each uyezd centre had two parts: the upper one, in red, with the exception of the Suzdal coat of arms, contained the lion, indicating that the town belonged to Vladimir Gubernia, and the lower one characterised the town and its uyezd.

There are specimens of the industrial products of the end of the 18th and the 19th centuries. The region was famous for its glass and renowned for its textiles: there are very attractive fabrics from the villages of the region.

Many items document rural life after the abolition of serfdom in 1861 in terms of livelihood, domestic life, and the crafts and seasonal work.

The exhibition concludes with the history of the revolutionary movement in the region. There are photographs of famous revolutionaries active in the area, a section dealing with Lenin's visit to Vladimir, and a display of pre-revolutionary editions of works by Marx, Engels and Lenin. The town of Gus-Khrustalny donated the type from one of the underground workers' printing presses at the beginning of the century.

The sections dealing with the town's history in Soviet times are in a separate building at 19, Mir St. (ulitsa Mira).

THE ASSUMPTION CATHEDRAL OF THE KNYAGININ CONVENT

Not far from Liberty Square, along Krasnomilitseiskaya St. stands the 16th century Assumption Cathedral of the Knyaginin (Princess's) Convent. At the turn of the 13th century Princess Maria Shvarnovna, wife of Vsevolod III, founded the royal Convent of the Assumption, called Knyaginin in honour of its founder, on this site. In 1200–01 the Assumption Cathedral was built in the centre of the convent, and served as the burial-vault for the female members of the royal family. Chronicles tell us that Princess Maria herself, Vsevolod III's second wife Anna, and the wife and daughter of Alexander Nevsky were buried here.

The old cathedral has not come down to us. The existing church was erected in the late 15th and early 16th centuries on the original foundations, thus making it possible to establish the appearance of the old cathedral. It was a single-domed, four-pillared church resembling the Cathedral of St. Demetrius. Unlike most Vladimir and Suzdal churches of that period, the building material was not white stone, but flat brick and the mortar including red-brick dust.

The new cathedral is basically a copy of the old one, but it was much altered by many accretions in different architectural styles. Only in 1960 was it restored to its 16th century shape, with the exception of the galleries which en-circled the cathedral in both its 13th and 16th century forms and have not survived.

The many tiers of the cathedral are very effective. Ornamental pilasters divide the walls into three, which culminate in two rows of ogee arch type *zakomary* gables. A ring of *kokoshniki** of the same shape encircle the bottom of the drum of the dome, and three portals with ogee arch type tops reinforce the unity of design. The motif was probably repeated on the covered galleries.

The cathedral is extremely spacious inside. The fact that the walls are not divided by pilasters, that there are no galleries, and that the pillars supporting the cupola have been moved towards the narrow side naves strengthen this impression.

The wall-painting has survived with the exception of that on the lower panelling. By the entrance the columns of the west portal are covered with intricate patterns of plant motifs. The church was painted in 1647–48 by a group of artists from the royal workshop led by Mark Matveyev, who had just completed work on the Moscow Cathedral of the Assumption. The northern wall, by the passage into the side-chapel, retains fragments of an inscription listing the painters' names. In the 19th century the frescoes were repainted following the old design. Now almost all the old murals have been uncovered, and restoration work continues.

---

* Kokoshnik—an imitation *zakomara* with a purely decorative function.

The murals are divided into several horizontal rows, each of which has individual scenes. We shall concentrate only on the most important of them. The dormition of the Virgin, to which the cathedral is dedicated, features on the exterior of the altar arch and the southern wall. The paintings on the altar section illustrate a number of episodes from the *Prologue*, a book of selected readings on the lives of the saints. The northern section of the altar depicts scenes showing the severity of the punishment administered by the higher orders of the clergy: the coffin containing the body of a priest, who is even a saint, must be removed from the cathedral during services until the punishment is remitted by the bishop. This fresco celebrates the power of the pillars of the Church, and preaches strict observance of religious discipline by the lower ranks.

The northern and southern walls depict many scenes and symbolic compositions in several rows from the acathistus of the Virgin. The upper section of the walls and the vaults have frescoes on the subject of the twelve main festivals of the Orthodox Church. There are portraits of prelates on the north-west pillar under the dome, and of Andrei Bogolyubsky, Vsevolod III, Konstantin and Georgi Vsevolodovich and Alexander Nevsky on the south-west pillar.

Finally, the *Last Judgement*, the largest composition, takes up almost the entire western wall. We have already seen fragments on the same theme in the Cathedrals of the Assumption and of St. Demetrius, and its treatment by painters of the 12th, 15th and 17th centuries illustrates the differences in their views of the world. In the Cathedral of St. Demetrius the main theme is that of retribution, of man's insignificance before the terrible godhead. Andrei Rublyov (1408) concentrates on the idea of redemption, the uplifted state of mind of people about to enter heaven (The Procession of the Righteous to Heaven). The 17th century painters were interested above all in the individual person, who occupies the central place in their compositions.

The *Last Judgement* in the Knyaginin Convent is characterised by the large number of people depicted and the many themes which run through it. It provides a panorama of the whole world, all earthly and heavenly forces. The painters show the movement in and the mood of the large crowd. The lower half depicts heaven and hell, and a large scaly dragon, with scrolls listing sins. Among the sinners stand some foreigners in breeches and white stockings, reflecting the church's opposition to foreign influence.

The colour combinations were carefully thought out: pale and dark green, deep blue, ochre, purple and maroon. This rich colour range enhances the refined forms and ornamental pattern work.

The frescoes are the most outstanding surviving example of Russian wall-painting from the first half of the 17th century.

The wooden houses around the cathedral recreate the atmosphere of pre-revolutionary Vladimir.

The Assumption Cathedral of the Knyaginin Convent

A fragment of a painting in the cathedral

Near the Knyaginin Convent, on the slopes of the ancient earth ramparts, stands the baroque **Church of St. Nikita** (Nikitskaya) (1762–65). Its building was financed by the merchant Semion Lazarev, and it is very different from other 18th century religious buildings.

Half of it is a secular structure: a three-storey palace with large windows and spacious rooms. The decorative details, the *nalichniki*, pilasters with capitals, volutes and cartouches contrast with the painted walls. The two-storey accretions date from the 19th century.

Making our way back from here to the trading centre (torgoviye ryady), we continue along 3rd International St. On the southern side of the street, almost opposite the trading centre, stands the former **Governor's House** of the 18th century. At that time the four-storey building was the tallest in Vladimir. In 1788 Admiral Mikhail Lazarev, the first man to explore the Antarctic, was born here.

The **Church of St. George** (Georgiyevskaya). Behind this building, on Krasny Profintern St., stands the baroque Church of St. George (1783–84) with its tent-roofed bell-tower, erected on the site of a 12th century white stone church. The present church was built partly out of material from the old church, dismantled after the 1778 fire.

One more block, and we turn left down Sovetskaya St. The unremarkable corner house on the right-hand (west) side once housed Vladimir's first cinema, which opened in 1907.

A fragment from the fresco, the *Last Judgement*

The church of St. Nicholas in Galei, 17th century

Churches of the Saviour (Spasa) and St. Nicholas (Nikóly). At the end of the street stands an attractive group of buildings. In the 12th century this was the site of Andrei Bogolyubsky's court with the Church of the Saviour (1164). It was rebuilt after the 1778 fire, and retains many of the forms typical of 12th century Vladimir and Suzdal architecture: walls divided into three sections, a belt of blind arcading, the portal with recessed arches, and plaster work in the guise of white stone blocks.

The 17th century Church of St. Nicholas, the smallest in Vladimir, standing next to that of the Saviour, is built according to the traditions of its age. A broad band of *kokoshniki* runs across the top of the façades, and the *nalichniki* are particularly ornate. Adjoined to the north-west corner is an original bell-tower, shaped like a square tower with a high spire, the niches of which are set with green tiles.

Vladimir today has approximately 500 streets. As we draw towards the end of our walk along the oldest and most lively of them, let us recall what a local regional historian said of it in 1877: 'The street is like an artery, drawing the life blood of the town to itself; here people shop, work, and attend entertainments. It is a substitute for Nevsky Prospekt and the Parisian boulevards, and provides a varied picture of the town's life in all its shades.'

This street was a part of the famous **Vladimirka**, along which thousands of fettered political prisoners were escorted on foot to Siberia. The road became the subject of many folk songs, Nikolai Nekrasov dedicated poems to it, and Isaak Levitan painted it. Vladimir writer Nikolai Zlatovratsky (1845–1911) describes in his memoirs the sight of a whole village of peasants, sent to Siberia by their landlord, passing through Vladimir: 'The crowd . . . bore down upon us like a huge wave. In the centre strode hundreds of men, old and young, lined into rows of several each, in a convoy of soldiers. Overtaking each other, sobbing and wailing, ran . . . women, dragging their children behind them; the soldiers shouted at them; people ran out from shops and some of the houses to give the peasants white and black bread, pies, and money; behind the people on foot came a long line of carts piled high with sacks and bundles of clothes, on top of which sat weeping women and small children; a thick cloud of dust hung over the entire street, through which rose the steady roar of various noises unspeakably unpleasant to the ear . . .'

3rd International St. comes to an end in houses with rounded corners. Buildings of this type are to be found in many Russian towns. When, in the 18th century, towns were rebuilt with regular planning, all residents in the central streets were required to build stone houses to conform to an approved plan. Minor officials and other small-propertied residents were invited to sell their homes and move to the outskirts. Even many of the wealthy were reluctant to part with their wooden homes. Ivan Betskoi, President of the Russian Academy of Arts, suggested to Catherine II that 'to start with, in each part of a town a corner house should be built, displaying two different façades to the whole street as models'. In this way people would see the indisputable advantages of stone structures. This two-storey building on the corner, belonging to Titular Counsellor Meshcheryagin, was such a model building. In 1795 it became the town post office, which it remained until 1918. Now the building houses various offices and an engraving studio. It was built in the last quarter of the 18th century by architect Ivan Chistyakov, at the same time as he was working on the reconstruction of the lower part of the Golden Gates. The round tower of the house resembles the Gates.

THE GOLDEN GATES

The Golden Gates (Zolotyie Vorota) are so much a part of Vladimir and its history that they have become the town's unofficial symbol.

The Gates were built in 1164, when Vladimir was striving to become the political centre of Rus and building was at its height. Andrei Bogolyubski, to enhance the prestige of the new capital, did his best to make it just as beautiful and rich in architecture as the old capital of Kiev, even to the extent of giving social places the same names. He therefore named the gates after similar structures in Constantinople and Kiev.

The Vladimir Golden Gates are truly unique both in Rus and in mediaeval architecture elsewhere. They united defence bastions and a triumphal arch: here troops were greeted and sent off, and honoured guests fêted. In 1252 the people of Vladimir welcomed Alexander Nevsky, their chosen prince, here.

The Golden Gates were an impregnable fortress when the situation demanded. Their strength was first put to the test soon after the death of Andrei Bogolyubsky, when internecine strife broke out between his nephews and his brothers. The Gates were stormed by the combined forces of Rostov and Ryazan. The town held out under siege for seven weeks, and surrendered only when food supplies ran out. Even Khan Batu was powerless before the Gates, and his men were able to break into the town only through a breach in the

wooden walls. The Gates stood up even to cannon bombardment in the early 17th century.

The repairs carried out after attacks gradually altered the Gates' appearance. In 1469 the Moscow builder Vasili Ermolin renovated the church above the gates. It was subsequently twice rebuilt, and its aspect is now that of the late 18th and early 19th centuries, when the Gates underwent their last, and most fundamental alteration. In 1785 the earth ramparts adjoining the Gates were removed to make way for a thoroughfare, and the walls, deprived of their support, had to be reinforced with counterforces enclosed in round towers. The battle platform around the church was altered into a covered gallery with windows instead of the former loop-holes.

Despite the later accretions, the Gates are a unique monument of the 12th century architecture and engineering.

The original part of the Gates is the mighty cube of the tower with a 14-metres-high arched passageway. Above the arch was the battle platform surrounded by a dog-toothed parapet. In the centre rose the church: it was traditionally held that a church above the town gates guaranteed the town divine protection. The Gates stood between strong earth ramparts, in front of which was a deep fosse. There are remnants of the ramparts to the south of the Gates (Kozlov Val). In 1966 a stone breast-wall was erected to prevent collapse of the ramparts.

Wooden gates, bound with gilded copper closed the passageway.

The Golden Gates, 12th century

The Military History Exhibition in the building of the Golden Gates: weapons from 1812 and a gypsum bas-relief by Fyodor Tolstoy

Hung on huge forged hinges they met at the centre of the lintel.

On the sides of the arch in the white stone masonry can be seen a groove and socket for the bolt which closed the gates, and also the upper pair of hinges. The lower hinges are now deep in the earth, for the 12th century road was $1^1/_2$ metres lower than the modern surface. There are large square niches in the pilasters of the support arches. They held the joists of the lower wooden battle platform.

Inside the south wall is a stone staircase in two flights, leading out onto the battlements. The lower flight comes to an end at the exit to the battle platform in the passageway. Graffiti, presumably scratched by 12th and 13th century soldiers, survive on the broad doorpost.

Among the crosses is the word 'Giurgich', which it is thought is in memory of the young Moscow prince Vladimir Yurievich, who was cut down by the Mongol-Tartars in full view of his brothers and the town defenders by the town wall.

The Military History Exhibition. The second flight of staircase leads to the upper battle platform and the church, where a museum was opened in 1956. It houses a diorama by Efim Deshalyt with sound-track on the people's defence of Vladimir during the Mongol-Tartar attack in 1238.

Material on military leaders connected with Vladimir and the surrounding area is displayed. There is a bust of Dmitri Pozharsky who led the home guards during the Polish and Lithuanian invasion at the beginning of the 17th century, it was designed by Mikhail Mikeshin in the 1860s. An anonymous serf artist from the 18th century is the author of one of the few portraits done of Generalissimo Alexander Suvorov in his lifetime. For several years he commanded the Suzdal Regiment and the Vladimir Division. From 1784 to 1786 he lived on his estate of Undol 30 kilometres from Vladimir.

Six home guard regiments were formed in Vladimir during the Patriotic War of 1812. With regiments from other towns, their duty was to defend Moscow and its surrounding area. An early 19th century engraving depicts General Piotr Bagration, who died in the village of Sima in Vladimir Gubernia from wounds sustained during the Battle of Borodino. In 1839 his ashes were transferred to the burial-ground at the scene of the battle.

The 1812 War inspired many artists. The museum has two gypsum bas-reliefs by Fyodor Tolstoy depicting *The Battle Near Krasny* and *Napoleon's Flight over the Niemen*, from his medallion series, which allegorically portrays civic patriotism.

The exhibits from the 1877—78 Russo-Turkish War include the banners awarded to the 9th and 10th Grenadiers for their defeat of the Turks near Plevna (now Pleven), some earth from the Shipka Pass, and the Order of the Bulgarian People's Republic naming the summit of the pass after General Stoletov (in 1951).

The exhibition also includes Russian and foreign weapons from various ages: poleaxes, hatchets, swords, curved Turkish daggers, muskets, and various kinds of rifles. A unique exhibit are the long (over $1^1/_2$ m) metal rods of the 13th century with pointed tip and three tail fans like an arrow weighing two kilograms. They were probably fired from a cross-bow type affair carrying inflammable mixtures.

The Gallery of Heroes of the Soviet Union. The gallery houses the portraits of 160 people from Vladimir awarded this title. It is in a room once used by the Gates guards.

The first person from Vladimir to be awarded this title on the 20th of April, 1934, was pilot Nikolai Kamanin, for his part in rescuing the crew of the *Chelyuskin*, crushed by ice in the Chukotka Sea.

The award was earned by many during the Great Patriotic War of 1941—1945. Lieutenant Alexei Lopatin had the title conferred posthumously: he commanded the outpost on the Western Bug, where for 11 days, until all the defenders were killed, the outpost repelled the enemy's superior forces. Pilot Nikolai Gastello, who before the war lived and worked in the ancient town of Murom, aimed his burning plane at a group of enemy tanks, petrol carriers and cars.

The award was given to 58 people from Vladimir for the liberation of Poland, Czechoslovakia, Hungary and Romania. Pilot Alexander Shornikov was in addition made a People's Hero of Yugoslavia for his evacuation in July 1944 of the Headquarters of the Yugoslav People's Liberation Army led by Marshal Tito.

Here too hangs the portrait of Vasili Degtyarev, Hero of Socialist Labour and outstanding designer of

Replica of an inn. The *Old Vladimir* Exhibition

Replica of a room in a wealthy townsman's home. The *Old Vladimir* Exhibition

automatic firearms. His light DP machine gun was as original, simple and reliable as the best foreign models. In 1941 his anti-tank gun played an important role in defensive battles near Moscow.

The last portrait is that of cosmonaut Valery Kubasov from the town of Vyazniki, twice Hero of the Soviet Union. In October 1969, as engineer on Soyuz-6, he performed the first cold welding of metals in conditions of natural vacuum and weightlessness; in July 1975 he took part in the Soyuz-Apollo Programme, and in May 1980 he flew into space with Hungarian Bertalan Farkas.

The display also includes the personal belongings of those who fought in the war, leaflets and posters, orders and medals, and samples of small arms designed by Degtyarev and other gunsmiths.

The Old Vladimir Exhibition. At the start of this century a water-tower was built to the south of the Golden Gates, at the top of the old earth ramparts. The tower, now obsolete, has been preserved because it marks a specific stage in the history of the town, and its three circular rooms now house the *Old Vladimir* Exhibition, depicting the town as it was at the turn of the century.

The main theme of the exhibition is Vladimir as a town of petty bourgeois, officials and merchants; Anton Chekhov once described Vladimir as the most boring of all Russia's provincial centres.

The exhibition plunges you straight back into those times. There are models of interiors from the home of a prosperous citizen,

a church sponsored shop, a police station, and an inn, with a traditional samovar, sugar-tongs, painted trays, old bottles, and carafes for vodka and brandy. Wall-paper in 19th century style, street lights and oil-lamps, and old advertisements all add to the atmosphere.

The usual explanatory notes to the exhibits are replaced with original excerpts from pre-revolutionary writings on regional history, thus providing in addition an opportunity to study the orthography of the time. Historians and journalists of the 19th century tell you about their town themselves.

Photographs, postcards, a door from an old mansion with an open-work awning and iron steps, cast-iron tethering posts, a firebell, clothing and other items are on display on the ground floor. Old street names reflect the local relief (Hill Street, Ilyinskaya Slope, Studenaya Hill), the social composition of the population (Gentry Street, Petty Bourgeois Street, Soldiers' Sloboda and Gendarme Hill), and the density of the churches, which gave their names to 27 streets. Here is an excerpt from the *Year-book of the Vladimir Gubernia Statistics Committee for 1880:* 'The town of Vladimir, once a town of major historical importance in Russia, is now, despite some traces of its former splendour still to be found in the old buildings, an ordinary Russian town, the modest administrative centre of a small but densely populated industrial gubernia.'

Old photographs show us Vladimir's aspect and its social contrasts. The central section of the main street was fairly respectable, with public buildings, the stone houses of wealthy merchants, and shops. Contemporaries wrote that 'the street could acquit itself well as a street in the capital'. In the other parts of the town stone houses were as rare 'as oases', and everywhere stood simple cottages with two or three windows inhabited by the poor; the streets were deserted and untended.

Next to the photograph of the Town Duma is a copy of its budget: a third was allocated to the upkeep of the police, courts and prisons; a quarter went to pay the town administrative staff, and the least proportion, 0.9 per cent, went on health care. Sums allocated to municipal services were so small that sometimes not a single street-lamp was working, or if they were lit they served only to 'darken even further the surrounding gloom'. The streets were extremely unhygienic. Only the fire brigade could serve as a matter of pride for the municipal authorities: of necessity, for there were as many as 200 fires annually in the gubernia. Next to the photographs of the town's fire brigade are the metal plaques of the societies providing insurance against fire with promotional names such as *Anchor* or *Hope*. They were affixed to the fronts of insured houses.

The clothing displayed reflects the lifestyles of various classes. The mantilla from a fashionable Parisian boutique belonged to a lady from the gentry, and the cashmere shawl was typical of a merchant wife's attire. Shop-assistants and workmen would stroll around the town in brightly-coloured shirts and smart caps with a large peak.

The first floor exhibition tells us about the occupations of the townsfolk. There are photographs of merchants, the clergy, the gentry, petty bourgeois, intellectuals, army officers and peasants. The only class not present are workers, because even in the latter half of last century the town's entire industry consisted of one small candle factory, to which were later added several equally unimportant brick factories.

The largest class was that of officialdom. A contemporary wrote: 'Government officials have put down their roots here, annually covering reams of paper, sending orders, circulars, memoranda, proposals and repeat notices to all the corners of the gubernia. Paid a pretty sum for their labours, the officials in turn let the rest of the population earn, and this interaction constitutes the pulse of the town's life.'

Fashion designers and tailors were among the most talented artisans, and displayed here is a Grand Prix diploma awarded to a Vladimir tailor at the Modern Age and Progress Exhibition in Paris in 1911.

Vladimir was famous for its coachmen, and although their number declined after the railway was built between Moscow and Nizhny Novgorod (now the town of Gorky on the Volga) in the second half of the 19th century, a contemporary could still write that 'the coachmen in Vladimir are skilled, and better than in the capital; wide carriages, tall horses, and they drive fast'. The smart sashes and special watches attached to the coachman's back on the sash, the bells with inscriptions which hung under the shaft-bows remind us of those bygone times of daring ˅coachmen, who were the favourite heroes in folk songs.

The second floor stands deal with religious and cultural life in pre-revolutionary Vladimir. Many photographs depict religious processions, groups of nuns, a preachers' society, and a priest teaching in a school. The church was a major influence in the town. Education was religiously oriented, and despite the existence of a considerable number of schools, the cost of tuition was prohibitive for many people. Statistics for 1880 tell us that there were 40 literate men and 25 literate women for every 100.

From newspapers we learn of the interests of the town residents with advertisements such as 'Young man prepared to marry any wealthy female in order to complete his education', 'Excellent card fortune teller'. A pack of cards exhibited next to other accessories for card games illustrates the importance of card games as a form of entertainment for the people of Vladimir. At the end of last century the number of packs of cards sold annually amounted to one for each resident.

Some theatre bills from 1901 are indicative of the Vladimir theatre's repertoire, mostly of a diverting nature. Next to the bills is a secret circular issued by the Vladimir Governor, forbidding the showing of films which might have a disruptive effect. The circular was inspired by the screening of a French film on the mutiny on the battleship *Potemkin* in 1905.

Let us complete our tour of the museum with a newspaper quote from 1878: 'Intellectual life in Vladimir is feeble. Reading is an activity held in reserve for killing time, and is a resort when there is no prospect of any more serious occupation such as a game of preference . . .'

At the top of the tower is a **viewing platform**, from which the old part of the town with its many monuments can be surveyed at a glance. The ancient architecture is seen as standing in little islands and also among later buildings. Beyond the old protected area modern buildings stretch in all directions as far as the eye can see, and even to the park beyond the Klyazma where the new hospital and hotel stand.

THE CHURCH
OF THE TRINITY

Next to the Golden Gates stands the former Old Believers' Church of the Trinity (Troitskaya), built in 1913–16 by local architect Sergei Zharov. Although the church lacks stylistic unity, it is interesting as the last church built in Vladimir and as a typical example of the search for new architectural means of expression at the start of this century. The church has been restored and now houses an exhibition of glass, miniature lacquered boxes and embroidery from Gus-Khrustalny and Mstera in the Vladimir Region.

The Exhibition. The first section covers the lacquered papier-maché boxes from Mstera, a large village on the River Klyazma, and renowned in the past as an icon-painting centre. Pedlars sold their icons throughout the country, but the craft began slowly to decline at the end of last century.

In Soviet times the best craftsmen turned their skills to producing lacquered caskets and boxes. The workshop founded in 1923 is now a large factory, whose products are always in demand and are displayed at exhibitions both at home and abroad. The Mstera painters still use the old Russian tempera technique of mixing their paints with egg yolk and vinegar.

Their methods differ markedly from those of the craftsmen of Palekh in Ivanovo Region, who use black almost exclusively as their background colour, whereas the Mstera painters depict their subjects against the background of nature in all its colours. Black is present only in the frame delineating the picture, and the colours are bright without being garish.

The artists find never-ending inspiration for their work in Russian history, fairy tales, epic songs, folk songs, and the work of great writers, especially Alexander Pushkin. The works fuse the distant past and the modern age, reality and fantasy: we see the white stone walls of ancient towns, boats rocking on blue white-headed waves, proud horses galloping, gay maidens dancing, and also the silhouettes of railway bridges and electricity pylons mingling in fantastic landscapes.

Among the works so varied in theme and style, the designs by Evgeny Yurin are particularly worthy of note. His bouquets of flowers and intricate patterns involve the skilled use of gold dissolved in aqua regia. His desk set is particularly original, with the inclusion of birds in the design.

A separate stand shows all the stages of the strenuous process of painting a casket, which takes approximately a month.

The glassware is displayed in the central section of the exhibition. It tells us of the history of glass production in the Vladimir area, and is indicative of the modern goods produced by the Gus-Khrustalny cut-glass factory.

In 1756 merchant Akim Maltsev from Oryol established a small glass factory on the River Gus, which soon became renowned for its wares. The oldest items shown here are the 18th century clear and opaque green bottles and pitchers. Simple in shape, they are reminiscent of earthenware vessels, and their soft outlines emphasise the pliancy and suppleness of the material.

In addition to the articles with smooth surfaces, where the impression was created by form and colour alone, soon glass vessels began to be decorated with relief applications, painting and engraving, as the beakers and bottles from the mid-19th century show. By the end of the century complex shapes had emerged, as well as faceted glass-stems. Gold painting also became a common decorative element. Cut-glass from the 19th century gleamed and sparkled like precious stones, hence the name of diamond faceting. The hookahs destined for the East are also worthy of note.

New decorative motifs appeared as the turn of the century, and shapes became mannered and unnatural. The glass was treated in such a way as to create an impression of a film of rainbow colours. Glass articles in imitation of other materials such as metal and bark were also manufactured.

The best traditions have been further developed in Soviet times. A widely adopted method is that of thematic diamond faceting, using motifs from the real world. The designs are reminiscent of frost patterns on windows, large drops of rain, the northern lights, and delicate lace work. Coloured glass in all shades is also common. The items exhibited are not merely utilitarian, they are also works of art, and the organ music which plays heightens this impression.

A lighting device in the centre of the room is a metal construction with crystal pendants in the form of balls and cylinders.

The third section on the first floor is devoted to embroidery, an ancient form of folk art, one of the largest centres for which was Mstera. As capitalism established itself this traditional domestic handicraft became a means of earning money: seamstresses made the trousseaux for the daughters of wealthy families. After the Revolution the Mstera seamstresses formed a workshop, which later became the Krupskaya Embroidery Factory.

The two different styles of Mstera embroidery are easily distinguished: one consists of delicate plant motifs in white satin-stitch made on white material; the other takes the form of 'Vladimir stitching', where the patterns include large fantastic flowers, birds in trees, cocks with fanned tails, and stylised female figures. The predominant colour is red, interspersed with yellow, green and blue.

Every Sunday the Chamber Choir of the Vladimir-Suzdal Museum gives a concert of old Russian music in the exhibition hall.

OUTSIDE
THE OLD TOWN

Most of the sights to be seen are in the old part of the town, but there are nevertheless some interesting buildings and exhibitions in the newer areas.

VLADIMIR
IN SOVIET TIMES

This is the continuation of the *Old Vladimir* Exhibition, and concentrates on social history and urban construction. The designers have abandoned the use of the conventional show-cases, where exhibits are seen in isolation. Here each theme is set in a context characterising the period.

Here, for example, is a reconstruction of a typical part of the town. Above the cobbled roadway with cast-iron tethering posts are suspended slogans such as 'Long Live Labour!' and 'The Red Army is the Shield of the Oppressed, the Sword of Those who Rise in Protest!' The posters on the notice-board announce discussions on religion and atheism. Among the material from the *Prizyv* newspaper is a decree on the renaming of streets whose names had religious or monarchic connotations, and the article 'You Won't Get Us on Our Knees', a reply to imperialist plots. Photographs show crowded meetings and large marches. Everything is imbued with the spirit of revolutionary

change with which Vladimir was charged in the early 1920s.

A model of building site reflects the socialist industrialisation of the 1930s. You feel that the workers have only just walked away, leaving behind them their wheelbarrows, overalls and tools. On the scaffolding hangs a leaflet urging everyone to come to work during Easter.

In 1928 the Vladimir power station brought electricity to the town, in 1932 the car appliances and chemical plants came into operation, and by 1937 Vladimir already had 47 industrial enterprises.

A school desk, blackboard, globe, textbooks for adults and club and theatrical announcements recreate the atmosphere of the efforts to eliminate illiteracy throughout the country.

The next interior takes us on to the time of the Great Patriotic War. It is a room in a typical Vladimir flat, with a simple table, bentwood chairs, book shelves, and a chest-of-drawers covered with a cloth on top of which stands a gramophone. On the walls hang portraits of Lenin and Stalin, children's drawings about war, and a black wireless, around which the family would gather to listen to the latest information, often read by Yuri Levitan, himself from Vladimir.

The exhibition also reflects the great industrial and residential construction after the war, and concentrates on events important in the life of the town: the first trolleybus

A lacquered box from Palekh

line opened, and the building of the bridge over the Klyazma. There is a special section devoted to the celebration of Vladimir's 850th anniversary, with a display of the gifts to the town from various regions and towns throughout the USSR.

The exhibition concludes with a look at Vladimir's future: here you can see models for blocks of flats, cinemas, schools, sports facilities and parks, and material on the restoration of ancient monuments. The exhibits are constantly renewed as the future becomes the present. The exhibition is at 19, Mir St., which can be reached on the No. 7 trolleybus, alighting at the Parkovaya stop.

THE INDUSTRIAL PRODUCTION EXHIBITION

The Vladimir Region is an industrially developed area, with altogether over 400 enterprises producing 6,000 items. Many of them are renowned, such as the hydraulic caterpillar excavators manufactured in the town of Kovrov, horticultural tractors, the Oka refrigerators made in Murom, and cut-glass from Gus-Khrustalny. Even before the Revolution the Vladimir country was famous as a textile area, and although now the major industries are mechanical engineering and metal processing, the region is still foremost in linen production, and third in cotton fabric production in the country.

The exhibition displays about 800 specimens of the industrial goods produced: tractors, pianos,

Cut-glass from Gus-Khrustalny

Mstera embroidery

radio equipment, furniture, car appliances, cut-glass, televisions, and artificial gems, in no way inferior to genuine precious stones.

The exhibition is at 47, Oktyabrsky Prospekt, which can be reached from the centre on trolleybuses Nos. 2 and 8, alighting at the stop Dom Kultury VTZ (the Cultural Centre of the Vladimir Tractor Plant).

ART GALLERY

The gallery houses the collection of the Vladimir-Suzdal Museum. The exhibition opens with a large portrait collection acquired in the 1770s and 1780s by Alexander Vorontsov, statesman and diplomat. It includes works by anonymous serf artists and canvases by the famous portraitists Ivan Nikitin and Fyodor Rokotov.

There is a selection of 19th century painting by such artists as Ivan Aivazovsky, Ivan Shishkin, Yuli Klever and Valentin Serov, representing the varied trends in Russian landscape painting. Particularly worthy of note is Alexei Savrasov's *Spring Day*, which in its simplicity of theme and its mood serves as a prelude to his famous *The Rooks Have Arrived*. In this everyday scene showing the outskirts of a village, the dirt road and puddles the artist conveys the poetry and beauty he sees in the Russian landscape.

Among the portraits Vasili Tropinin's *The Lace Maker* stands out as one of the first examples of the transition from salon portraiture to the depiction of everyday life.

Social themes are dealt with by Alexei Venetsianov in his *The Soldier's Story* and Leonid Pasternak in his *In a Train Carriage*.

Heroic lays and folk tales served as a source of inspiration for Viktor Vasnetsov, and the gallery has a version of one of his most famous paintings, *After Igor Svyatoslavich's Battle with the Polovtsi*, inspired by *The Lay of Igor's Host*. In keeping with traditional folk imagery, the steppe grass is flattened, dark storm clouds carry the sad news home, and eagles quarrel over the prey. The solemn silence of the recent battle field conveys the magnificence of the military deed and the reverence of all the people of Russia for the fallen heroes.

The gallery houses some important Soviet painting: landscapes by Stanislav Zhukovsky, Nikolai Romadin, Vitold Byalynitsky-Birulya, and portraits by Boris Kustodiev, Fyodor Modorov, and others. Konstantin Yuon's large canvas deals with the first achievements of Soviet aviation. Ivan Kulikov from Murom was attracted in his work to the life of the peasants. Paintings from the 1940s to 1960s represent various themes and styles.

There is a wide selection of paintings by modern artists from Vladimir, such as Vladimir Yukin, Kim Britov, Valery Kokurin and Nikolai Modorov. Their works reflect the beauty of their native country, and have been exhibited in Italy, the GDR, France, Czechoslovakia and Japan.

The gallery is situated in the Park of Vladimir's 850th Anniversary, and can be reached from the centre on trolleybuses Nos. 1 and 8, alighting at the stop called Kolkhozny Rynok.

TRADESMEN'S QUARTER

To the east of the middle section of old Vladimir lay the suburb, or *posad* where the tradesmen and artisans lived. Tourists usually pass through this area on their way to the sights outside the town by coach.

The old buildings here were exclusively of wood, and the small square was surrounded by several wooden churches. The local inhabitants, engrossed in their everyday affairs, led very insular lives. The empty, crooked streets filled with people only when the ringing church bells announced a service: regular attendance was considered a sign of moral uprightness and respectability.

The streets and squares here were also lively during festivals. Ball games and *gorodki* (a kind of skittles) were played, the girls sang songs and young lads tested their strength against each other. In winter the favourite amusement was tobogganing.

In the 17th century, when the wave of stone building swept all Russia, the wooden churches were gradually replaced by new brick ones.

THE CHURCH OF OUR LADY

The most remarkable of these brick churches, the Church of Our Lady (Bogoroditskaya), lies on our route. It was built in 1649 by the 'labours and zeal' of several rich merchants. By this time the tastes of the merchant class had begun to determine the basic traits of Russian architecture. Mediaeval austerity and simplicity gave way to fanciful shapes and ornate decoration, and the Church of Our Lady is an excellent example of this trend.

The tall base divided by pilasters culminates in three rows of *kokoshniki*, from above which rise, like the stamens of a flower, five cupolas on narrow, intricately decorated drums. Originally each dome was covered with shingle. The refectory joins the church and the attractive two-tiered bell-tower. Covered galleries extended to the north and west, and two ornately decorated porches provide the entrances to the church.

The compositional complexity, the many tiers of *kokoshniki* and the abundance of architectural detail make the Church of Our Lady an important and typical example of 17th century Russian architecture. The architect, by using the great decorative potential of the brickwork, managed to avoid the excessive ornamentation which was common at the time.

THE FORMER SEMINARY

The long three-storey building built in 1860–63 to house the seminary concealed the attractive view of the Church of Our Lady and its ensemble. The front of the building is in late Russian neo-classical style. Although the seminary's function was basically to train members of the clergy, many of its former pupils decided upon secular careers. Some of its most telented pupils became major figures in the world of culture. Timofei Osipovsky (1765–1832) was a mathematician with progressive views. Vukol Undolsky (1815–64) became famous as a collector and student of manuscripts and old printed books. His authoritative *A Study of Slavonic-Russian Bibliography* which lists 4,705 editions of books in Cyrillic script printed from 1491 to 1864, is still of interest today.

The seminary produced several famous regional historians, including Alexander Smirnov (1854–1918), the author of a five-volume study of people renowned in various walks of life who hailed from Vladimir country.

STATUE OF MIKHAIL FRUNZE

Where Frunze Street (ulitsa Frunze), the continuation of 3rd International St., comes out on to Frunze Square, (Ploshchad Frunze), the coach crosses the boundary of ancient Vladimir, which ran along the bank of the Lybed. Here, in the 12th century, by the bridge over the river, stood the Silver Gates, where in 1174 the people of Vladimir waited to pay their last respects to the body of Prince Andrei, murdered by conspiracy in Bogolyubovo (see p. 90). The gates have not survived, and now the river flows underground. The statue of Mikhail Frunze stands on the approximate site of the gates. The monument to the hero of the October Revolution and the Civil War, the work of sculptors Boris Yakovlev and Yuri Vashkevich, was unveiled in 1974. 'Mikhail Frunze's life story reads thus: work in the underground movement, the barricades, the death-sentence cell, hard labour camp, the Revolution, the command of revolutionary troops and glorious victories,' wrote *Pravda* on the day of his death in November 1925.

Frunze spent several years of his eventful life in Vladimir Gubernia. In 1905 he was among the leaders of the striking weavers in Ivanovo-Voznesensk and of the first Soviet of Workers' Deputies. He was arrested in 1907 and imprisoned in Vladimir's main prison. He was twice sentenced to death, the sentence being eventually commuted to hard labour.

Never did Frunze allow himself to lose heart, and even in his cell awaiting execution he studied English and Italian. In addition to the street and square, one of the town's districts is named after him. The statue was erected with the finances and participation of the Komsomol organisation in Vladimir.

THE MILITARY CEMETERY

Our route leads on past the old town cemetery, a large area of which is taken up by the military cemetery, where the soldiers who died in Vladimir's hospitals from wounds received in the battles of the Great Patriotic War are buried. An avenue of blue spruce leads to the memorial to them, where an eternal flame burns. Every year on Victory Day, the 9th of May, a procession moves slowly from the town centre to lay wreaths here.

Beyond the cemetery, along the Rpen, lay fields with the ancient names of Prince's Meadow and Yarilo's Valley*. As late as the end of last century festivities which harked back to ancient Slav rituals were still held here, almost ten centuries after the introduction of Christianity.

Now Vladimir's industrial zone occupies the Rpen valley. We pass the Research Institute of Synthetic Resins, the Avtopribor and chemical plants, and the chimneys of the thermal electricity power station.

---

* Yarilo—the pagan god of sun and fertility.

Statue of Mikhail Frunze

VLADIMIR'S
EASTERN DISTRICT

Here the industrial landscape gives way to the new residential district which has grown up over the last 15 years. It is bounded by Dobroselskaya St., the ring road, and the road to Suzdal. The blocks of flats are built largely according to stereotyped plan from pre-fabricated reinforced concrete blocks and panels. Most of the houses are nine-stories high of different shapes. Along Rastopchin St. (ulitsa Rastopchina) stand groups of nine-storey tower blocks interspersed with long five-storey blocks. Recently buildings of more complex shape have begun to appear: one of them stands on the junction

Memorial to those who died during the Great Patriotic War (1941–45)

of Dobroselskaya St. and Suzdalsky Prospekt.

The new district is provided with shops, cultural and service facilities, schools, play-schools and crèches. The upper stories of some of the blocks of flats are given over to artists' studios.

In its expansion the town has engulfed several of the nearby villages. The oldest of these, Dobroye, is now contained within the Eastern district, and has given its name to Dobroselskaya St. On the right-hand side of the street, opposite the turning to Suzdal, is a large hospital complex, occupying a whole block. A little beyond it rise the five domes of the 18th century church, built on the site of the ancient Monastery of Sts Konstantin and Elena (Konstantino-Eleninsky).

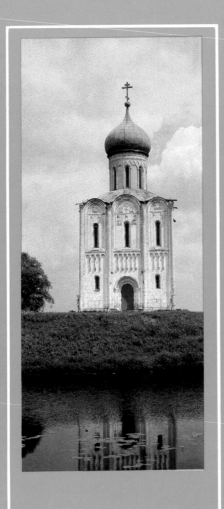

TRIPS
OUTSIDE
VLADIMIR

There is much of interest in the vicinity of Vladimir, and foreign tourists are usually offered trips to Bogolyubovo and Suzdal, both places renowned for their interesting architecture. Intourist coaches are provided and tourists are accompanied by local guides with an in-depth knowledge of the area. The excursion to Bogolyubovo takes two hours, the one to Suzdal a whole day.

THE STONE AGE SETTLEMENT OF SUNGIR

To the east of Vladimir the road to Bogolyubovo crosses a deep gully called Sungir, a pre-Slav name the meaning of which has not been elucidated. A stream which flows into the Klyazma gurgles along the bottom, and the slopes are overgrown with oaks, aspens and hazel bushes. A field slopes gently down to the gully, and rye, oats and potatoes are grown here in the summer.

Nobody suspected that three metres below the surface a layer of soil still contained the remains of a settlement which stood here

about 25,000 years ago. The settlement was almost at the edge of the receding glacier, and its inhabitants hunted reindeer, polar foxes, wild horses and hares. Mammoths still roamed in the tundra forests, but they were gradually dying out.

The Sungir settlement was discovered in 1956 during studies of the quarry here, which provided clay for the local brick factory. Excavations, led by historian Otto Bader, continued for 20 years. Over 4,000 square metres were explored, and the finds included the remains of camp fires, the hollows dug for fires, the sites of six ruined dwellings, tens of thousands of stone items, many bone objects and articles made of shells.

Sungir is distinguished both by the quantity of finds, and their scientific importance. The flint implements found here have much in common with those discovered in Stone Age settlements on the Don, and indicate that cultural links between Stone Age people extended over vast distances of what is now the European part of the USSR.

The burial site discovered here is of particular value, unique in its wealth of items and the complexity

Archaeological findings in the Stone Age settlement of Sungir

of the burial ritual. One grave was found to contain the skeleton of an elderly man, the other those of two adolescents, a boy and a girl, laid out head to head. Mikhail Gerasimov, renowned Soviet anthropologist and sculptor, has reconstructed the appearance of these ancient people from the surviving skulls. A complete set of ornaments was discovered: bone bracelets, rings, brooches, amulets in the form of flat sculpted animal figures, strings of beads, reflecting by their position on the skeletons the shape of the clothing which has not survived. It is reminiscent of the attire of the peoples of the Far North today.

The grave of the adolescents contained about twenty daggers, javelins and spears made of straightened mammoth tusks. The longest spear is 2.42 metres, and these spears are the first of their kind ever to be found. We do not yet know how these people, living at the very dawn of civilisation, managed to straighten such resistant material.

The flat sculpted animal figures are the most ancient works of art to be found in North-Eastern Europe, and the ornamental rows of dots, grouped in distinct patterns, show that even in Paleolithic times people had a counting system.

The Sungir discoveries also serve to reveal the gaps in our knowledge of how Stone Age people lived. It would appear that by this time man had acquired many skills, was fairly well attired, and better armed than we had previously thought. His ideological conceptions had acquired a certain complexity.

The studies of Sungir involved archaeologists, geologists, anthropologists and paleolithic botanists, and have led to numerous articles and books, and a film. The interest of both experts and the general public has led to a museum pavilion being erected here, which will soon house an exhibition on the settlement, which is of key importance for the study of the Paleolithic Age in the Russian Plain.

As the coach continues southeast it begins the steep climb up the hill to the nearby 11th–12th century town of Bogolyubovo, one of Vladimir's ancient outposts, surrounded by a ring of mighty earth ramparts and fosses.

The staircase tower of Andrei Bogolyubsky with a triple window and a belt of blind arcading, 12th century

BOGOLYUBOVO

Bogolyubovo occupies an important place in the history and culture of the Russian people. It is spread out on the high slope overlooking the Klyazma valley, with a good view of the twists and turns of the river's course and the forests beyond the river. The remains of the magnificent 12th century buildings take us back to the turbulent and tragic reign of Andrei Bogolyubsky.

Bogolyubovo was founded in 1158 with the building of the Cathedral of the Nativity of the Virgin as a political move crucial in Andrei's campaign for autocracy. From its position on the high bank of the Klyazma near its confluence with the Nerl, the fortress surveyed the main waterways of the region, thus drastically curtailing the independence of the local boyars.

Prince Andrei, in order to avoid any clashes with the feudal lords, had to make the siting of the fortress here appear an act of necessity. His supporters devised a story which attributed Bogolyubovo's founding to Prince Andrei's obedience to the divine will. The legend runs that the horses, on which the prince was transporting the 'miracle-working' icon of the Virgin from Kiev to Rostov, stopped still on this spot and refused to budge. That night, in the camp he struck here, the Virgin Mary herself appeared to Prince Andrei, desiring him to keep the icon in Vladimir, and to build a church consecrated to her on the spot where the horses had stopped. This legend gave rise to the name of the fortress (Bogolyubovo means beloved of God), and the prince became known as Andrei Bogolyubsky.

Chronicles record that Andrei built for himself a town of stone, but as no stone fortifications survived, and as the walls of old Russian towns were usually of wood, this information was considered dubious. In 1954, however, during excavation work led by Nikolai Voronin, the foundations of 12th century white stone walls were discovered at the top of the western rampart.

The mighty fortress was built over the years 1158–65. The fortifications, forming a fairly regular rectangle, extended for over 900 metres. In the centre, stood the Cathedral of the Nativity of the Virgin, compared at the time to that of Solomon, and the prince's chambers, joined to the cathedral by a covered gallery. Descriptions in chronicles in conjunction with archaeological studies make it possible to reconstruct Bogolyubovo's original aspect.

The comparatively small one-domed church was built of hewn white stone blocks. Its façades culminated in *zakomary* gables and were decorated with carving; the portals were bound with gilt copper. The interior was ornate and original: the walls were covered with finely painted murals with extensive use of acanthus leaf patterning, the floor was of large, gleaming copper flags, and the usual cross-shaped pillars supporting the dome were replaced with imitation marble columns with gilded capitals.

The throne beyond the low altar gates bore a canopy, and a chronicler wrote in admiration that it was designed with great imagination. The decoration also included gold and silver vessels and expensive materials. The icon of the Bogolyubovo Virgin, painted for the cathedral and now in the Vladimir-Suzdal Museum, is an invaluable work of Russian art.

Priest Mikula, the prince's comrade, wrote in his story of Andrei's death, that he liked to take his guests, Russian and foreign traders and ambassadors, up to the galleries, so that, astonished by the wealth of the cathedral, they would spread the word far and wide of the might of Vladimir's ruler.

The square in front of the prince's chambers and the cathedral was paved with stone slabs, and on the site of the present 17th century brick tent-roofed chapel stood an eight-pillared Holy Canopy made as a type of summerhouse. The canopy sheltered a stone bowl for holy water on a three-stepped pedestal. One of the pedestal blocks retains the mark of the principality, indicating that local craftsmen took part in building it. Legend has it that when Prince Andrei used to pay the palace builders, he drew the money from this bowl. Now the surviving fragments of stone paving and foundations of the Holy Canopy lie beneath one and a half metres of subsequent layers.

Bogolyubovo, with its golden-domed churches, white stone chambers, galleries, spiral staircases, sculptures and painting was a magnificent ensemble of its time, and what survives provides us with unique examples of 12th century architecture.

Bogolyubovo saw not only the beginning but also the tragic end of Andrei's reign in Vladimir. The prince's stern temper, and his ambition to create a centralised state provoked the important boyars, led by the Kuchkovichs, to conspire against him. A chronicle vividly describes the events. On the night of the 29th of June, 1174, twenty conspirators cut down the prince's guards, and tried to enter the prince's bedchamber, one of the conspirators attempting to pass himself off as the prince's favourite servant Prokopy. When their ruse failed, they began to break down the door. The prince leapt from his bed and reached for his sword, only to find that the steward had taken the precaution of removing it. By this time the conspirators had broken in; in the darkness they cut down one of their own men, taking him for the prince, but they soon discovered their mistake. They then set upon Andrei, dealt him many wounds, and left him for dead. There was still life in the prince, however, and he crept out of his bedchamber and down the spiral staircase to hide in the alcove behind the eastern pillar. There the conspirators found and killed him.

Now only the remnants of the earth ramparts, overgrown with age-old limes and elms, a section of the fosse which has been turned into a pond, and the few surviving fragments of the white-stone buildings remind us that Bogolyubovo was once a royal residence. The section in the best state of repair is the steep arched passageway and the staircase tower, above it an 18th century tent-roofed bell-tower. They share the same decorative elements: a belt of blind arcading, which, evidently, ran round all the main façades, binding them into a single whole.

The eastern wall of the tower has an attractive triple window divided by columns with carved capitals, while more ornate carving adorns the capitals of the corner semi-columns. Inside the tower is round. The stone steps of the spiral staircase, lit by four narrow windows at different levels, lead up to the passageway, the walls of which have 18th century murals depicting the murder of Prince Andrei. Monks in olden days would pass this passage off to pilgrims as the bed-chamber where Andrei was mortally wounded.

In actual fact the royal bed-chamber was to the north of the staircase tower, in the northern wall of which you can see the filled doorway which led to the prince's chambers. For a long time it was held that the tower was joined to the chambers by a wooden gangway, but excavations have discovered the foundations of a second arched passageway in the ground. One's glance is caught by hewn stones, dark with age, bearing the marks of an archway and narrow, scarcely visible windows. These are the remains of the prince's chambers: the part that connected the chambers and the cathedral.

The lower half of the cathedral, uncovered during excavation work, has been left exposed to reveal the attic socle of the western wall, and the foundations of the round pillars supporting the dome, on which now stand the pillars of the present church.

The exhibition in the 19th century cathedral helps us to picture the appearance of the buildings. It contains details of both the interior and exterior decoration, large photographs and reconstructions of objects and frescoes. Of special note is the large block, on each side of which is depicted a female head, that of the Virgin Mary. It is thought that this capital was either part of the cathedral entrance, or crowned the Column of Our Lady, which stood before the cathedral entrance. Another interesting exhibit is an example of 12th century script, a large white stone cross with a carved inscription which stood in bygone days at the mouth of the Nerl as a channel marker.

Bogolyubovo soon declined after this brief period of prosperity. Shortly after Andrei's death it was badly damaged by the Polovtsi led by Prince Gleb of Ryazan, and in 1238 it was destroyed by the Mongol-Tartar hords.

Eventually a monastery was established in the surviving buildings. It was surrounded by a brick wall with seven towers, the entrance being through the Holy Gates with their belfry built in 1841. Finally in 1866 the vast five-domed Cathedral of the Assumption was erected in conventional Russian-Byzantine style. The houses which had grown up around the monastery gradually developed into a large village. Its inhabitants were farmers who also engaged in icon-painting and other crafts. The local roof-makers and plasterers were driven by need to seek work in distant parts of the Russian Empire. Fairs were held here every September.

Today Bogolyubovo is a small settlement with a fruit-canning plant, part of the local brick-making factory, a printing press, shops, cultural centre, restaurant, hospital, secondary school and other institutions for children. Bogolyubovo has about 50 hectares of orchards.

The Bogolyubovo architectural monuments are part of the Vladimir-Suzdal Museum.

THE CHURCH OF THE PROTECTING VEIL ON THE RIVER NERL

One and a half kilometres from Bogolyubovo the Church of the Protecting Veil (Pokrova), renowned in world architecture for its perfect proportions, stands amid a broad flood plain on the bank of the River Nerl.

The church was built in 1165 on Andrei Bogolyubsky's behest. We have already noted that his attempts to bolster his power involved making use of the worship of the Virgin Mary, who, it was claimed, guided all his undertakings. The church is consecrated to the festival of the Protecting Veil, unknown in Byzantium; it is thought that it was first introduced by Andrei to enhance the prestige of the Vladimir-Suzdal Principality in its rivalry with Kiev.

This new festival had its origins in the Byzantine legend of the appearance of the Virgin to a local saintly fool, supposedly called Andrei, in the church on the Hill of Vlachennae in Constantinople. He saw the Virgin, hovering in the air, take off her cloak and spread it over the people as a sign that they were guaranteed her protection against natural disasters and enemies. In Vladimir, aspiring to become the capital of all of Rus, the miracle was interpreted as a sign of the special divine protection afforded to Prince Andrei in his unification policy. *The Lay in Praise of the Protecting Veil of the Mother of God* contains a prayer to the Virgin Mary for protection against 'the arrows flying in the darkness of our division'.

In Ancient Rus major events were usually marked by the building of a church. The Church of the Protecting Veil, built in just one summer, was a celebration of Andrei Bogolyubsky's victorious campaign in Bulgaria on the Volga.* Victory was mingled with grief, for Andrei's eldest son Izyaslav died of wounds received during the campaign.

The Church of the Protecting Veil is reached on foot, across soft green meadows wrapped in silence. Across the path stands a group of old elms, and you glimpse the church through their trunks. Once past the trees, the small single-domed church is revealed in all its glory on a slight hill at the very edge of the water. Gleaming white, it seems to have been sculpted from a single lump of white stone.

Its typical 12th century shape astonishes by its faultless proportions and the purity and sharpness of its outline; only the best Ancient Grecian architecture can compare with it in this respect.

The architects were intent on conveying an impression of light-

ness and grace, the church's slender height giving it an ethereal quality. The church is slightly longer than it is wide. The triple apse is gently rounded. The walls incline slightly inwards, which adds to the impression of height. The same effect is achieved by the division of the façades into three equal sections by elegant pilasters, the narrow windows, and the belt of blind arcading. Everything contributes to the vertical lines. Above *zakomary* gables rises the graceful drum with its cupola.

Seen from a distance, the church is an unforgettable sight. At close quarters, its details are fascinating. The drum has fine columns by the windows, and a band of dog-toothed triangles, a typically Russian pattern, with a row of protruding bricks above. The carving on each wall is, in keeping with mediaeval tradition, of a symbolic nature. The complex meaning of each composition has not yet been fully elucidated, but the general import is clear. It is linked to the consecration of the church to the Protecting Veil of the Mother of God, and to the idea of peace and unity under the aegis of the 'divinely chosen' prince.

The central figure on each of the three façades is that of Old Testament King David, seated amid the beasts and birds of prey he has tamed. The side sections of each wall show gryphons, not tearing a doe to pieces, as sometimes interpreted, but rather sheltering it with its wings. Modern theory sees these reliefs as symbols of the divine protection afforded to the righteous.

---

* The first state formed by the peoples of the Middle Volga and the Kama (10th-mid-15th centuries).

Slightly lower, just above the windows, is a row of female heads, unique in its harmony. They are thought to be either symbols of the Virgin Mary, or to represent the people to whom she affords her protection. Lions, symbols of princely power and guardians of the church, are depicted near the central window. Halfway up the columns of the blind arcading have patterned consoles. The arches of the portals are also carved.

The single reliefs and small compositions on the Church of the Protecting Veil are the first steps on the brilliant road of Vladimir-Suzdal carving, which led to the magnificent sculptural ensembles on the Cathedral of St. Demetrius.

The interior of the church may at first sight seem disappointing: there are no ancient frescoes (the last traces of which disappeared at the end of last century), no iconostasis or golden treasures. But you soon involuntarily fall under the spell of the architecture. You forget that the church is empty. Here, even more than from the outside, you sense the height of the church. Your eyes are drawn upwards through the light well of space between the four pillars, slightly narrowed at the top, supporting the dome.

The bottoms of the wall pilasters are adorned with twenty pairs of carved lions with human expressions on their faces: some bear a cunning grin, others a self-satisfied grimace, and yet others bare their ugly, crooked teeth in a furious roar.

It is usually held that the lions of the interior, too, are the symbols of princely power, but the unprepossessing appearance of the beasts somewhat contradicts this theory. Georgi Wagner suggests instead that they are the symbols of evil forces defeated by heaven. The expressions of the beasts bear witness to the acute power of observation and tendency to caricature of the sculptors.

People come from all over the world to see the Church on the Nerl. Miles of film are expended on photographing it, much has been written about it in both a learned and popular vein, and all the poems dedicated to it would fill a sizeable book.

Since the first articles by regional historians written over 100 years ago, not one piece about the church fails to stress its unique situation and harmony with nature. Indeed, the church seems to belong naturally in the landscape.

It looks particularly beautiful in springtime, when the hill on which it stands is a tiny island in the midst of the floodwaters. We now know that this hill is man-made, and that originally it was paved with white-stone slabs which have not survived. It is thought that the church, perfect as it seems to us today, looked different 800 years ago. In 1954—55 archaeologists discovered foundations for an unknown structure within the hill. Nikolai Voronin is of the opinion that they are the foundations for galleries which once surrounded the church on three sides at a

The Church of the Protecting Veil on the River Nerl

distance of $2^1/_2$ metres from the walls.

The white facing of the hill and the presumed arched gallery would have greatly enhanced the church's grandeur, more in keeping with Andrei Bogolyubsky's desire to make every one of his buildings worthy of a capital city. But the church will always be remembered as it is today—small and intimate, and so perfect that the addition of a single stone would spoil the harmony of its proportions.

SUZDAL

Tourists visiting Vladimir invariably include Suzdal in their itinerary as well. Suzdal is a small town 35 kilometres to the north of Vladimir, and as famous for its architecture. The road to Suzdal passes through an undulating, almost woodless plain, a mysterious fertile island of dark earth typical of more southerly latitudes.

For centuries the main occupation was cereal farming, and the Suzdalians produced enough wheat to feed themselves and supply other towns. With time, however, the fertility of the soil declined, and by the early 20th century the area was considered to be one of consumption rather than production in agricultural terms.

Fertility has been radically improved, and now the land yields unprecedented harvests of up to 4,000 kg a hectare. The area also specialises in market gardening and livestock-rearing.

A wide belt of orchards stretches along the road for several kilometres. Despite frequent severe winters, fruit has been grown in the area from time immemorial. In spring the landscape is white with cherry blossom, and warmed by clusters of rowan berries in autumn.

Some old villages stand on our route from Vladimir to Suzdal. Just outside Vladimir, to the left of the highway, *Sukhodol*, at least 500 years old, nestles in a small valley. We know that in 1515 Prince Vasili Ivanovich obliged his peasants in the village to bring tribute of rye, wheat and peas, and money to pay for salt and firewood, to the Cathedral of St. Demetrius.

On the high bank of a small stream stands *Borisovskoye*, mentioned for the first time in 1328 in Ivan Kalita's royal testament.

The last village we pass through is that of *Pavlovskoye*, which already stood on this site in the 13th century. Now it is the centre of the large Frunze State Farm, which has roughly 10,000 hectares of arable land. Residential construction for its 2,000 inhabitants is going ahead, with two-flat brick cottages with out-buildings attached, and blocks of 14 to 18 flats of the urban type with cellars for storing vegetables and preserves. They will have land for vegetable gardens and orchards attached. Sectional barns are going up nearby for privately-owned livestock and poultry. Other facilities will include a school, a shopping centre, a club with a cinema and a large library, restaurant, sports centre with a swimming pool, and a park.

Suzdal is ten kilometres further on from Pavlovskoye. Suddenly you catch a hazy glimpse of cupolas, towers and belfries, which grow ever more distinct. Suzdal is one of the most ancient of the old Russian towns, so old the meaning of its name has been lost. It is first mentioned in chronicles in connection with the anti-feudal uprising in 1024 in the Rostov-Suzdal Principality, at the north-eastern limit of the Kievan state. By the mid-12th century it was a major political centre, the capital of an independent principality with its kremlin, a fortified *posad*, and the country residence of Yuri Dolgoruky, the first sovereign prince of Rostov and Suzdal.

His son, Andrei Bogolyubsky, as we know, made Vladimir his capital, and the principality became known as the Vladimir-Suzdal Principality, where Suzdal retained a special position: in an attempt to counteract separatist tendencies it for a long time was not made an appanage principality for the younger princes, and remained in the possession of the Vladimir prince. Only in the early 13th century did the town become an independent principality.

In 1238 Suzdal was pillaged by Khan Batu, but recovered, and in 1262 its inhabitants joined with those of other towns in North-Eastern Rus in rebelling against the invaders.

In the 16th century, after a long interval, stone building began here on a large scale, largely prompted by the Moscow tsars who found ideological backing in the history of ancient Suzdal.

The first half on the 17th century was a time of trial and tribulation for the town. In 1608 to 1610 it was twice raided by Polish and Lithuanian invaders, after which only 78 houses remained in the *posad*. The town had hardly recovered from this blow when it was plundered in 1634 by Tartars from the Crimea. Ten years later a terrible fire destroyed the area of the town next to the kremlin, and in 1654—55 plague carried off half of the town's population, then standing at less than 2,500.

Building continued despite all

these troubles, and the main architectural ensembles which have come down to us already existed by the end of the 17th century.

Under Peter I, when major monastery building was curtailed because of the construction of St. Petersburg, intensive building began in the *posad*, financed by rich merchants. The many *posad* churches, standing very close to one another, make Suzdal so distinctive today.

Suzdal was not untouched by the town planning measures taken by Catherine II's government, which affected over 400 towns and cities in the Russian Empire. In 1789 plans laying out the main streets, squares and residential quarters were approved. The partial implementation of this plan led to a marked delimitation of the population. The poor were pushed out to the edge of the town, as only those who could afford to build a two-storey stone house were permitted to live in the centre.

In 1796 Suzdal became the centre of one of Vladimir Gubernia's uyezds, and acquired its own coat of arms: a falkon in a prince's crown on a red and blue background. Unlike other towns under Vladimir, the shield did not depict the royal lion, a tribute to the town's former autonomous status.

The 19th century was not marked by any ensembles or buildings equal to the architecture of previous centuries. In 1806–11 Alexei Vershinsky designed a shopping arcade similar to many others in small provincial towns. Neither is the Empire-style bell-tower of the Monastery of the Deposition of the Robe (Rizopolozhensky) particularly outstanding.

Until the mid-19th century the trade route to Arkhangelsk and St. Petersburg lay through Suzdal, and the local merchants prospered. With the building of the Moscow-Nizhny Novgorod (now Gorky) railway, however, its trading importance declined, many cottage industries closed down, and the population fell. The main occupation became market gardening, and remained so until 1917.

'Each town,' wrote Nikolai Voronin, expert on Vladimir and Suzdal culture, 'has a specific function to fill. One may become an industrial giant, another a centre for science. Suzdal's future lies in its past, preserved for the generations to come.' Soviet restorers have given Suzdal architecture a new lease of life, and it is an important part of the national heritage. This is true also of the white stone carving, painting, and applied art which can be seen as an inherent part of the architecture in the ancient churches, and at exhibitions.

In no other Russian town do so many monuments from all ages of Russian history survive in such a fine state of preservation, and Suzdal is with every justification called a museum town.

In 1967 the Council of Ministers of the USSR passed a resolution to build a large tourist centre with hotels, camping sites, motels, restaurants, museums and souvenir shops in Suzdal. As many as a million Soviet and foreign tourists stay here every year.

On the 20th of August, 1974,

Suzdal was awarded the Order of the Badge of Honour for its contribution to the preservation of the national heritage and restoration of ancient monuments, and in commemoration of its 950th anniversary.

The obelisks of the Vladimir Gates (19th century) mark the entrance to Suzdal. At this point begins Lenin St. (ulitsa Lenina), the main thoroughfare, which runs through the whole town, coming to an end by the identical obelisks of the Yuriev Gates. Small houses, often with carved *nalichniki*, behind them gardens and orchards, line the road. Off it branch narrow tree-lined streets.

As you walk around the town, you are struck by the skill of the Suzdal architects. Wherever they built, whether on a steep river bank or on a low plain, their churches always blend with the landscape and the nearby buildings.

THE KREMLIN

It is best to begin one's tour of Suzdal with the kremlin, the ancient citadel situated within the bend of the River Kamenka. The fortress, surrounded by earth ramparts extending for 1,400 metres, was built here at the turn of the 12th century. A deep fosse was dug along the neck of the isthmus on which the fortress stood, thus making it effectively an island.

Along the ramparts ran log walls with towers. They were destroyed several times, but always rebuilt, right up to the early 18th century, when the last fortifications, put up in 1645, were razed in a large fire.

The Cathedral of the Nativity of the Virgin (Rozhdestvensky sobor). This is Suzdal's oldest surviving church, built in 1222–25, although it has not come down to us in its original form. Only the lower part of the walls, finishing at the belt of blind arcading, remains from the 13th century building. Above it the walls were relaid in the 16th century, when brick replaced the original white stone.

The many 17th and 18th century alterations destroyed the old galleries, widened the windows, and drastically changed the interior. For more than two centuries the cathedral stood with an unnatural flat, sloping roof on four sides. Finally, in the 19th century, the façades with their carving were plastered over and painted red. It took a great deal of work to restore both the cathedral and

The Cathedral of the Nativity of the Virgin in the Suzdal kremlin

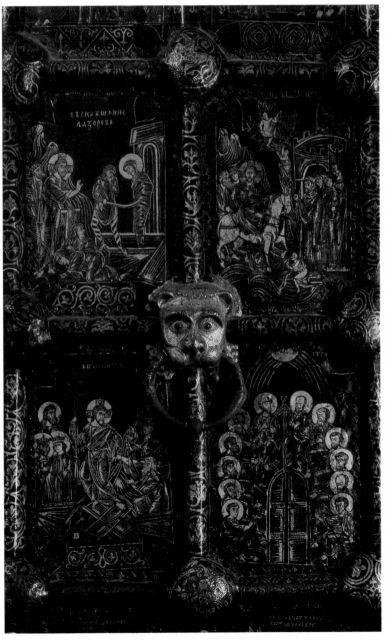

The western ''golden gates'' of the Cathedral of the Nativity of the Virgin

A fragment of a mural in the cathedral, 13th century

other kremlin buildings to their original appearance.

The cathedral is famous for its two 'golden gates', made of copper sheets etched with acid and then gilded. The west doors portray scenes from the Gospels and have the first depiction in ancient Russian art of the Protecting Veil of the Mother of God. The south doors illustrate the lives of the angels, and in particular of Archangel Michael, the patron saint of the old Russian princes in their military undertakings.

Other items deserving of attention are the 17th century lamp in the shape of a five-domed church for use in religious processions, and the splendid chandelier, a gift from Prince Ivan Shuisky.

The Suzdal princes and archbishops were buried in the cathedral.

The cathedral was first painted in 1233 by local artists. The most important of the surviving fragments are in the upper section of the south apse, depicting the figures of two senior monks with stern, ascetic faces. The painting is both precise, and yet graceful and subtle. There is extensive pattern work, and the figures of the saints are somewhat lost among the intricate designs.

The fragments of the 1635–36 murals are extremely valuable. The later over-painting has been removed from them in the north and south entrances and on the right-hand west pillar. The 17th century five-tiered iconostasis, one of whose authors was Grigory Zinoviev from the royal workshop, has been recently restored.

After a tour of the cathedral

you can listen to recordings of old Russian music.

The Bell-Tower. An enclosed square lies in front of the cathedral, bounded to the south by the 1635 bell-tower, the earliest example of 17th century Suzdal architecture. A tent roof surmounts the octagonal base. The highest building in the town, it was a distinctive landmark. In the late 17th century a clock, which chimed the hours, quarter hours, and even minutes, was mounted on it.

The Archbishop's Chambers. The triple-span arched passageway of the bell-tower connects with the Archbishop's Chambers, restored by Alexei Varganov. The establishment in the second half of the 15th century of an independent eparchy in Suzdal led to the building of residential quarters for the clergy, a private church, and other essential structures. In 1688–1707, under the Suzdal Metropolitan Illarion, an eminent figure in the church, those buildings from various periods were combined into a single, vast and involved complex, which contains many features typical of 17th century architecture: the attractive arrangement of the various components, the galleries, impressive portals, richly decorated *nalichniki*, and the use of coloured tiles. The main entrance to the chambers, opposité the cathedral entrance, has a conical tent roof covered with green tiles. A broad staircase in two flights lead to the reception hall, the Cross (Krestovaya) Chamber, 13 metres wide and 26 metres long. The roof is a closed vault without supporting piers, and it is an outstanding example of the skill of the Suzdal architects. It was the source of universal admiration. Paul of Aleppo in Syria wrote in his notes about his travels in Russia in 1654–56 that it was 'a piece of architecture of great rarity . . . which has no equal, even in the tsar's palace'.

The vault was dismantled in 1874, and even before that the chamber had been divided into several rooms. Now its original appearance has been restored, and an 18th century interior reconstructed in it. Worthy of note are the stoves, dating from that time, with painted tiles of various shapes.

The many rooms of the chambers now house several permanent exhibitions of the Vladimir-Suzdal Museum.

The Leninist Policy of Preserving Historical and Cultural Monuments. This exhibition deals with the restoration and museum work in Vladimir Region, as we know one of Russia's most ancient historical and cultural centres. Millions of roubles are spent on restoring the more than 900 monuments discovered and placed under protection. This is just one example of how the Soviet state protects the people's historical and cultural heritage. Lenin saw the introduction of general public to this heritage as one of the conditions necessary to create a new socialist culture. It is to promote Lenin's aims that the Vladimir-Suzdal Museum was founded, an amalgamation of all the thirteen historical, memorial and art museums in the area.

Suzdal is one of the finest examples of the preservation and promotion of the cultural heritage, a museum town, and an international tourist centre.

Suzdal's History. The exhibition opens with a display of archeological finds which tell us about Suzdal's emergence as a trading, craft, political and cultural centre in North-Eastern Rus. There are many items by local potters, bone-carvers, smiths and casters. Among the finds are articles from other areas, which give us an idea of Suzdal's trading links: an amphora of apparently southern origin, weights for a spindle made of argillaceous schist from Ovruch near Kiev, bracelets from Novgorod, pieces of fabrics from Byzantium, Arab coins, and much more besides.

There is a display of Russian and Tartar weapons from the early 13th century, both originals and models. The Mongol-Tartar invasion greatly damaged Vladimir-Suzdal economy and culture. The tragic events of that time lived on in people's memories and were later depicted by the local anonymous artist who illustrated the manuscript of **The Life of St. Evfrosinia of Suzdal** (17 century).

The painting and applied art of the 14th and 15th centuries from Suzdal's monasteries show that despite periodic destruction Suzdal continued to retain its importance as a cultural centre for a long time, and Moscow in its early days made full use of the town's heritage.

Among the clothing, utensils, and rich treasures from monasteries

The main entrance to the Archbishops' Chambers (in the Suzdal kremlin)

The Cross Chamber

are a child's shirt and small white tombstone from the 16th century. The story attached to them is a mysterious one. In 1526 Tsar Vasili III exiled his first wife Solomonia Saburova to Suzdal's Convent of the Protecting Veil (Pokrovsky Monastyr) because she had not borne him any children. When he married his second wife Elena Glinskaya from Poland, rumours from Suzdal claimed that the disgraced princess had given birth to a son called Georgi. He was said to have died soon, and been buried in the Convent of the Protecting Veil. In 1934 the grave was opened, and some bundles of rags from a decayed doll dressed in a silk shirt were discovered. Whatever the motives for this false burial, people were reluctant to give the tale a sad conclusion, and the legend arose that Solomonia had managed to save her baby, who grew up to be the good robber Kudeyar.

A remarkable example of book production is the manuscript copy of the Gospels from 1614, bound with chased silver sheets and set with precious stones. The last page bears the signature of Dmitry Pozharsky, leader of the home guard in 1612.

The high quality goods produced by local smiths, copper-smiths and casters reflect the economic revival of town in the 17th century. The display includes examples of Russian leather, morocco and printed fabrics which were Suzdal's main export items.

Until the latter half of the 18th century the monasteries were a major economic force in Suzdal. The increasing exploitation to which serfs were subjected on monastery lands caused many of them to flee. When they were caught, such instruments of punishment as fetters, collars and branding-irons, displayed here, were used.

The museum's exhibits include a glass chandelier, trunk and table belonging to Evdokia Lopukhina, Peter the Great's first wife, and prisoner at the Convent of the Protecting Veil. She had been brought up in the traditions of the past, and could neither understand nor accept his innovative changes. She was forcibly made to enter the convent as a nun.

The show-case dealing with 18th century culture contains books and documents from Suzdal's first seminary, founded in 1723. Its pupils included Dmitri Vinogradov, who was responsible for creating Russian china. The exhibits from the 19th century are mostly items used by merchants and peasants in their daily lives.

Old Russian Painting. This exhibition of 13th to 17th century icons consists mostly of local works, collected, studied and restored in Soviet times. Before the Revolution they were not readily available to art students, to say the least, and Goethe, to his inquiry about old Suzdal icon-painting in 1815 received the official reply that there was no such thing in Suzdal.

The specific features of Vladimir and Suzdal icons are their compositional precision, refined contours, contemplative style, and soft colour range. The Suzdal traditions were the ones which the Moscow school, which grew up in the 16th century, chose to develop.

The oldest icon here is that of **Our Lady of Maximovo**, painted in 1299 in connection with the removal of the metropolitan's office from Kiev to Vladimir. Although time has left its mark on the icon, it shows clear signs of the pictorial style which was later to become the hallmark of the Vladimir-Suzdal school.

The icon of **Our Lady of Eleusa** (15th century) still retains a certain Byzantine influence in the lengthened proportions, delicate facial features and introspective expression. However, it has more immediacy and warmth than similar Byzantine icons.

The Annunciation (15th century) is one of the first examples of the work of the Vladimir-Suzdal school. It is a good illustration of Igor Grabar's description of Suzdal icons as 'the art of fine proportions, graceful lines and fantastically intertwined designs'. This small (29 × 23 cm) icon, dynamic with its rhythmical lines and elegant colours, has great emotional impact.

The icon of **The Protecting Veil** (late 15th-early 16th centuries) from the cathedral of the Convent of the Protecting Veil, stands out for its inspirational qualities, perfect composition, colouring using similar shades, and fine ornamental elements. The depiction on the icon, on the cathedral window, of the lion, the symbol of the Vladimir and Suzdal lands, indicates its local origin.

Works of great individuality can be found within one artistic school, and this is true of the 16th century icon of **St. Nicholas with Scenes from His Life**, an original folk variation on the theme, with its fiery red, bright blue, golden, white and green colouring.

The icon of **St. Nicholas with Chosen Saints** from the 15th century is an example of the influence of other schools on the Suzdal painters. The red background and a certain austerity in the depiction of the figures is indicative of the possible influence of the Novgorod school.

In the 20 two-sided 16th century miniature icons from the Cathedral of the Nativity the soft lines typical of the best icons of the Vladimir-Suzdal school are less evident. They are of an illustrative nature, based on scenes from the Gospels, and contain some narrative elements which were to become widespread in the 17th century.

A walk around the earth ramparts is recommended before you leave the kremlin. They provide a view of the Kamenka, the *slobodas* (settlements) beyond the river, and the monasteries and churches with which the remainder of the tour will acquaint you.

THE POSAD

The road from the Kremlin leads to the *posad* and several 18th century churches as worthy of attention as the ancient architecture we have just seen. Suzdal church architecture of that time was characterised by a small cube topped by a four-sided sloping roof replacing the *zakomary* gables. The large windows and absence of piers supporting the cupola make the interiors light and airy.

Church of the Resurrection (Voskresenskaya). The church (1720) stands with its classical purity and austerity in the square before the shopping arcade (torgoviye ryady, formerly Gostiny dvor).

The bare walls, devoid even of *nalichniki*, add to the impact of the cornice of small *kokoshniki* and the south porch built in 17th century tradition. The church's central position in the square is emphasised by the tall bell-tower, ornately decorated with rows of niches inset with coloured tiles. Suzdal architects were particularly adept at creating decorative contrasts between churches and their bell-towers.

A group of well-integrated buildings from different times stands on the northern edge of the former *posad*, consisting of the five-domed **Church of St. Lazarus** (1667) (Lazarevskaya) and the single-domed **Church of St. Antipa** (Antipievskaya) (1745) with a richly decorated bell-tower.

This combination of a large summer church, small winter church and tall decorative bell-tower was typical of Suzdal in the 17th and early 18th centuries. This was the time when the *posad* and *slobodas* were going up, and such pairs of churches, often with a concave-tent-roofed bell-tower, also typical of Suzdal architecture of the time, are common in the town.

THE MONASTERY OF THE DEPOSITION OF THE ROBE (RIZOPOLOZHENSKY)

Just beyond the *posad*, in the highest part of the town, stands the Monastery of the Deposition of the Robe, first established in the 13th century. No buildings earlier than the 16th century have survived, and the two worthy of note are the triple-domed church in austere 16th century style, and the Holy Gates with their twin tent roof built by local craftsmen Ivan Mamin, Andrei Shmakov and Ivan Gryaznov in 1688. The façade, with its two archways of different sizes, is decorated with inset coloured tiles. The tent roofs stand on octagonal bases. With their deceptive simplicity and grace the Holy Gates are considered one of the town's best pieces of architecture.

The tall multi-tiered bell-tower was erected in 1813–19 to commemorate the victory over Napoleon. The construction of the bell-tower, with its yellow walls with white details, was presided over by local stonemason Kuzmin.

If you are in Suzdal when the weather is warm, the 40-metre-high bell-tower affords an entrancing view of the town, the peaceful, winding Kamenka, and the open spaces of the surrounding plain.

THE ALEXANDROVSKY MONASTERY

A little to the north of the Monastery of the Deposition of the Robe stands the Alexandrovsky Monastery, founded, according to legend, by Alexander Nevsky in 1240 on the bank of the Kamenka. The earliest surviving buildings are from the 17th century. The construction of the Church of the Ascension (Vozneseniya) (1695) was financed by Tsarina Natalia Naryshkina. It is a big structure, tastefully decorated with details we have already encountered; a portal with recessed arches, edged like the *nalichniki* with white stone 'beads', and a row of graceful *kokoshniki* on the cornice. The bell-tower built at the same time is more austere: it is the only octagonal base in Suzdal which is completely bare.

The churches of St. Lazarus and of St. Antipa with the bell-tower

THE HOUSE
IN THE POSAD

On the northern edge of the town, also on the bank of the Kamenka, stands the Monastery of Our Saviour and St. Euthimius (Spasso-Evfiemiev). Our route towards it passes the house in the *posad*, Suzdal's only surviving example of residential architecture from the late 17th and early 18th centuries, now No. 134 Lenin St. (ulitsa Lenina). It consists of two sections of different heights with separate gable roofs. Additional eyebrow-shaped decorations crown the *nalichniki*.

Restoration in 1971 was followed by the reconstruction of interiors similar to those which existed in the latter half of the 18th century, when the house was owned by Ivan Bibanov, baker and restaurateur. The old furniture, iron-bound trunks, large copper cauldron, mortar for grinding grain, vats, wooden buckets, copper and earthenware crockery, icons, popular prints hung on the walls for a decorative effect, and other items (altogether about 160) help to recreate for us the life of the *posad* residents, to whose work and tastes Suzdal owes much of its appearance.

The Holy Gates of the Monastery of the Deposition of the Robe

Alexandrovsky Monastery, windows decorated with white stone "beads"

THE MONASTERY OF OUR SAVIOUR AND ST. EUTHIMIUS

The monastery is one of the oldest in Suzdal, founded in the mid-14th century by Prince Boris Konstantinovich of Suzdal and Novgorod. Later major donations of serfs and land, money and other treasures were made by Vasily III, Ivan the Terrible, the Pozharsky princes, and others.

In 1678 the monastery owned over 10,000 male serfs. The monastery's wealth made it possible to undertake major construction, resulting in a complex of 16th and 17th century stone buildings which replaced the wooden structures, and provide a fascinating example of Russian architecture of that time.

In the 1670s the monastery was surrounded by a mighty wall with 12 towers, a fine piece of military engineering, at the same time richly decorated with various mo-

tifs in keeping with the traditions of 17th century Russian architecture. The most impressive of the towers is the 22-metres-high Proyezdnaya (Entrance) Tower, with its loop-holes framed by ogee arch shaped *nalichniki*, and decorated with a row of niches and other details.

The Church of the Annunciation. The main buildings of the monastery are reached through a small courtyard beyond the tower and another gateway, surmounted by the 16th century Church of the Annunciation (Blagoveshchenskaya), which at first had a twin tent roof, and is now crowned with a small cupola. The varied and elegant decorative features include wide cornices, patterned *nalichniki*, and icon-case of ogee arch shape above the archway. The *nalichniki* of the porch windows are reminiscent of the recessed arch portals of 12th and 13th century Vladimir and Suzdal architecture.

Cathedral of the Transfiguration of Our Saviour. A shady pathway leads from the Church of the Annunciation to the Cathedral of the Transfiguration of Our Saviour (Spasso-Preobrazhensky sobor) (1594), the monastery's central edifice. Its decorative details also reflect the traditions of 12th and 13th century local architecture and consist of a belt of blind arcading and portals with recessed arches.

The murals inside the cathedral have survived almost intact. They were executed in 1689 by a group of painters from the ancient town of Kostroma, led by the renowned

The house in the *posad*, a monument of 17th–18th century civic architecture

Walls and towers of the Monastery of Our Saviour and St. Euthimius

Entrance Tower of the Monastery of Our Saviour and St. Euthimius

The Church of the Annunciation

Guri Nikitin and Sila Savin. The frescoes, covering a multitude of subjects, are typical of the 17th century narrative tendency, accompanied by explanatory inscriptions. The overall effect is of a coloured patterned carpet or the pages of a richly illustrated book.

The vast iconostasis from the cathedral, dating from the 1650s and constructed in celebration of the monastery's 300th anniversary, is now on display in the Andrei Rublyov Museum of Ancient Russian Art in Moscow.

Near the eastern wall of the cathedral is Dmitri Pozharsky's grave.

The Bell-Tower. This nine-sided pillar topped with a gallery with a triple-span arcade for the bells stands next to the cathedral. Building work went on over the 16th and 17th centuries. The decorative features, consisting of niches, balusters, and interlocking *kokoshniki* join the different parts into a single whole. The triple tent roof which crowned the bell-tower in the 17th century was later dismantled.

The Refectory Church of the Assumption (Uspenskaya). This church, erected in 1525 and standing opposite the bell-tower, is of great interest as one of the earliest examples of tent roof architecture. It adjoins the two-storey Archimandrit's Chambers, the five rooms of which house an exhibition of books from six centuries: manuscript books from the 15th century onwards, and printed books from the 16th to 20th centuries.

Manuscript books richly decorated with miniatures and illuminations show the high level that the art of book ornamentation had reached in Old Russia. The book most worthy of attention is the version of the Gospels of the late 17th century from the Cathedral of the Nativity of the Virgin. It has a sumptuous silver binding, engraved by Afanasy Trukhmensky, renowned craftsman from the Armoury in Moscow.

The collection of printed books opens with the *Book of the Apostles*, produced in Moscow in 1564 by the first printers Ivan Fedorov and Piotr Mstislavets. Of interest are the *Legal Code* of 1649, listing the laws of the Russian state establishing serfdom, the *Russian Grammar* by philologist Melety Smotritsky (1648), which accepts as official usage some elements of the spoken Russian language in Old Church Slavonic, and the *Large Primer* (1694) by Karion

Cupolas of the Cathedral of Transfiguration of Our Saviour

The Church of St. Nicholas and a hospital block

Istomin, Russian poet and one of the first Moscow educators. The latter has copper engravings by Leonty Bunin, and is the first illustrated textbook in Russia. Books printed in Kiev stand out for their ornate title-pages. The strong cultural links between the Ukrainians and Russians led to these books being widespread within the Moscow state. The selection of 18th century books is varied, with works on military matters, geography, history, philosophy, and other subjects. This period includes works by scientists Mikhail Lomonosov and Vasili Tatishchev issued during their lifetime, the first Russian edition of Don Quixote, and the first books published in Vladimir. There are also examples of the work of Nikolai Novikov, the most important publisher of the 18th century.

The 19th century editions of literary works published during their

The Book of the Apostles, 1564

author's lifetime include the first collection of Alexander Pushkin's poems, issued in 1826, and now of great rarity value, and two books by Alexander Herzen from his Free Russian Printing House in London.

The exhibition concludes with a display of pre-revolutionary and early Soviet editions of works by Marx, Engels and Lenin.

The Prison Block. A prison with individual cells for religious and political dissenters was founded in the monastery in 1764. The single-storey block was separated from the main complex of the monastery by a high brick wall. Imprisonment was for life, and the list of prisoners included, apart from Old Believers and other religious sectarians, minor officials, soldiers, actors and serfs. In 1829 Decembrist Fyodor Shakhovskoi was transferred here from Siberian exile, and here it was that he died, after refusing to eat as a sign of protest. One of the cells here was earmarked for Lev Tolstoy. The prison was closed down in 1907. Now the building houses an exhibition entitled Prisoners of the Monastery Jail.

The Church of St. Nicholas. Next to the prison block stands the Church of St. Nicholas (Nikolskaya) with a two-storey hospital block from the 17th century. Now it houses an exhibition of over 500 works of applied art from the 13th to 20th centuries: examples of decorative casting, stone, wood, and bone carving, and articles of gold and silver adorned with precious stones, pearls, coloured enamel, chasing and engraving. Some of them were locally made, others were royal gifts to Suzdal monasteries.

The small collection of miniature sculpture from the 13th to 16th centuries is first-class, consisting mostly of small icons, crosses, and panagias (images worn around the neck by Orthodox bishops). It also includes two Byzantine cameos of the 11th and 12th centuries

The pall with a portrait of
St. Evfrosinia of Suzdal, 16th century

in fine gold frames of Russian origin.

The gold and silver icon frames are of considerable interest. The most typical motifs are stylised flowers, contained within luxuriant twisted stems, the combination of smooth and matt scales, each with a rosette, and a filigree pattern of large volutes with fine loops. The frame of the *Corsun Icon of the Mother of God* (1509) is one of the finest examples of niello work on silver.

The exhibition boasts two cunningly made 16th century chandeliers: one is round, entirely covered with plant motifs, while the other is in the shape of a cubic single-domed church and decorated with chased symmetrical patterns which include the clover leaf and flower buds.

A unique item from the first half of the 16th century is the pall bearing a portrait of Saint Evfrosinia of Suzdal. It is not brightly coloured, nor is it decorated with precious stones, but it astonishes by its profound depiction of character. Evfrosinia's bearing and slender figure, her inspired expression of concentration, seem to embody the features typical of Russian women.

Two palls with portraits of the Suzdal bishops Ioann (1578) and Fyodor (1581) are brilliantly embroidered. The clothes are richly embellished, the faces delicately embroidered, and the silken stitches so expertly placed that they seem to have been carefully painted on with a fine brush.

Each item on display is convincing proof of the talent inherent within the people, of their inexhaustible imagination and skill. The exhibition gives us an idea of the basic stages in the development of Russian applied art, and its variety both where style and genre are concerned.

Museum of Amateur Art of the Peoples of the RSFSR. The Brothers' Cells, where the museum is housed, were until recently considered to be among the newer buildings in the monastery, but during restoration work it was discovered that the ground floor dates back to the 17th century, and that the upper storey was added in the 19th.

The museum, the first of its kind in the RSFSR, was opened in 1977, and displays exhibits of the most varied kind produced by our contemporaries in their leisure time.

They include jewellery, chasing, wood and bone carving, articles made of birch bark, earthenware and straw toys. The show-cases also contain woven wool from Bashkiria and Udmurtia, multi-coloured embroidery from Mordovia, painted fabrics from Tataria, and the brightly coloured national costumes of the peoples of the North and Far East.

The exhibition also includes varied works by amateur artists: some of them reflect the traditions of peasant art, others try to imitate renowned artists. The works by primitivists are very distinctive. This trend, one of the major representatives of which is Ivan Nikiforov from the Moscow Region, is characterised by the sharp expressive qualities of the image, a child-like immediacy of perception, deceptively simple composition, unusual dimensions, and bright, sharp patches of colour.

The Convent of the Protecting Veil

THE CONVENT
OF THE PROTECTING VEIL

From the high bank of the Kamenka by the Monastery of Our Saviour and St. Euthimius there is a fine view of the Convent of the Protecting Veil (Pokrovsky) founded in 1364. The first buildings there were of wood, and the ensemble as we see it today took shape in the 16th and 17th centuries, when the convent acquired many generous royal gifts of land, and became the place where women of the aristocracy were exiled for life as the result of dynastic or family conflicts, and the rigid customs of the time.

The Holy Gates. The main entrance to the convent was through the Holy Gates in the south wall, with the Annunciation (Blagoveshchensky) Church (1518) above them. Here Suzdal architects masterfully combined elements of church and fortification architecture, and decorative folk details. The large arched passageway is slightly to the right off centre, leaving room for a narrow archway for pedestrians on its left. Open-arch galleries surround the small three-domed church on three sides. The façades of the gates bear small niches and belts of protruding bricks.

The Office Building. Inside the convent, to the left of the gates, is the office building from the early 17th century. The long single-storey building is divided into three rooms: the records were kept in the central room, the one on the right housed the convent archives, and

The cathedral and bell-tower of the Convent of the Protecting Veil.

the left room was reserved for conducting interrogations and inflicting corporal punishment. Beneath this room is a small stone cellar where the guilty were kept.

An 18th century interior has been recreated in one of the rooms according to information from the convent inventories.

Cathedral of the Protecting Veil (Pokrovsky sobor). The cathedral (1510–18) forms the majestic central edifice of the convent. The large four-piered church with its imposing triple apse and open gallery stands on a high base, which once contained the burial vault. Gently sloping wide steps lead up to the gallery, through the arcade of which can be seen the smooth white stone walls of the cathedral. The belt of blind arcading, the only decorative feature, runs along the walls at a height greater than that of the gallery roof. The three cupolas are asymmetrically placed, the central one on its mighty drum being particularly impressive.

Inside, the walls were never painted, and the austerity was relieved only by rows of icons, which included some veritable masterpieces, richly embroidered fabrics, and precious vessels.

The Bell-Tower. The bell-tower, of which only the lower half survives with original decorative features, was built at the same time as the cathedral. The space housing the bells and the tent roof were added in the 17th century. The older, lower part contained a minute church, beneath which, as beneath the cathedral, was a burial-vault. In the 18th century the cathedral and bell-tower were joined by a gallery, with two arched passageways beneath.

Refectory Church of the Conception (Zachatievskaya). The two-storey refectory church to the north of the cathedral, built in 1551 at the behest of Ivan the Terrible, is very distinctive.

The refectory itself, in the shape of a vaulted square with one supportive pier, is on the first floor. The church is adjoined to its east side, and on the west is a hall with a staircase leading to the ground floor, which housed various auxiliary premises.

The refectory differs from the other earlier convent buildings by its diamond-shaped pattern of small red bricks on the cornice, which is typical of Polish, not Russian architecture. It is possible that Polish craftsmen were involved in the construction of the refectory. Next to it is an unusual hexagonal bell-cote, unusual because this shape appeared in stone architecture only in the 17th century. On it was mounted a clock which chimed the hour.

Although the Convent of the Protecting Veil fulfilled the depressing role of a women's prison, its architecture is nevertheless original and inspired.

The convent now houses a hotel, which is comprised of wooden cottages, similar to those in which the nuns once lived.

Church of Sts Peter and Paul (Petropavlovskaya). Opposite the Holy Gates, in the former Nikolskaya sloboda which the convent once owned, stands the large five-domed Church of Sts Peter and Paul (1694). It now houses an unusual exhibition, the focal point of which is the Jordan Canopy, a unique 17th century construction in the shape of a summer-house edged with figured boards painted in many colours.

A jordan was the name given to a temporary wooden chapel built over a hole in the ice where water was sanctified and ritual bathing took place during the festival of the Epiphany. The Jordan Canopy was built and painted by serfs from the Convent of the Protecting Veil and Archbishop's Residence. It is of great interest as a part of the 17th century way of life and a typical example of painting on wood from that time and unique as the only surviving structure in Russia.

THE MUSEUM OF WOODEN ARCHITECTURE AND PEASANT LIFE

Suzdal is so fascinating a town that visitors often do not notice the chronological gaps in the architecture, and yet fortress walls, the homes of the boyars and princes, and the houses in the *posad*, in fact all buildings of wood, have been lost to us. This prevents us from forming a complete picture of the way our predecessors lived.

Special open-air museums have been established in order to preserve the few examples of wooden architecture that survive today, and one of them is to be found in Suzdal. The first exhibit appeared in the town in 1960, brought from the village of Glotovo. This is the **Church of St. Nicholas** (1766); it was put up in the kremlin. This rare example of a church, reminiscent in shape of an ordinary peasant's dwelling, was followed by other wooden structures from all over Vladimir Region. They were sited in a special area on the left bank of the Kamenka, where once the Dmitrievsky Monastery stood. The Museum of Wooden Architecture and Peasant Life is structured as a village street of houses, churches, and various other buildings.

Attention is always attracted by the **Church of the Transfiguration** (Preobrazhenskaya) built in 1756, from the village of Kozlyatyevo. Built in tiers which diminish in size, and topped by an onion cupola, it is slightly reminiscent of a bushy fir-tree.

The former convent courtyard, now the hotel grounds

Next to it stands the **Church of the Resurrection** (Voskresenskya) dating from 1776 from the village of Potakino, and in comparison a simpler building. The sanctuary, main cube, bell-tower and west porch are all built along one axis, like a ship. The bell-tower is original, with its framework widening towards the top, a tradition dating back to the distant past.

To the west lies a street of log houses with out-buildings. The 19th century house from the village of Ilkino is a typical example of how middle peasants lived at that time. It is a sturdy house raised high above the ground, with a gable roof of planks. Carving in the old style adorns the front. The planning, with the living quarters, enclosed porch and store-room, is typical of the 19th century.

The interior of that time has been recreated inside. To the left of the entrance is the Russian stove, which was used for heating the room, cooking, and drying grain; it also served as a bed and often a bath-house. The woman had her corner in front of the stove, where she cooked and kept her kitchen utensils. To the right of the door is the man's work bench, where he would repair footwear and harness, make wooden articles for the home and farm, and rest when his labours were done.

The 'red corner' in the front of the room contains a table and icon-case. Wide benches line the wall, and here in the evenings the women would spin flax or sew.

The house from the village of Log, built in the mid-19th century, belonged to a prosperous family and is illustrative of the profound changes in the peasant way of life after the abolition of serfdom in 1861. It has an urban-type cornice, and the lower floor houses three looms: by the mid-19th century home weaving had become a form of capitalist production. A carved wooden bed replaces the usual work bench, and is a symbol of prosperity.

Middle-aged local people still remember the carts which used to transport grain to the windmills, although not one now functions in or around Suzdal, or anywhere in Vladimir Region. The last two surviving windmills, from the village of Moshok, now stand here in the museum.

The museum completes its picture of peasant life with other utilitarian structures: a 'stepping well' from the village of Koltsovo, where the large cogged wheel was turned by treading on its steps, a barn for drying sheaves before grinding, and granaries on stilts from the Oka valley, which always flooded in the spring.

The wooden Church of Transfiguration, built in 1756

Wood was not just a building material: it was also used to make carriages and sleds, looms and spinning wheels, crockery, utensils, and musical instruments. All these objects are on display in the museum. Each exhibit, whether a church or a wooden scoop or salt-cellar, displays the ability of the people to combine practical qualities with beauty.

The museum has both enhanced Suzdal's appearance, and filled the missing gaps in its architectural history.

A part of the Museum of Wooden Architecture

KIDEKSHA

Many tourists also visit the village of Kideksha, four kilometres to the east of Suzdal, on the edge of which, on the right-hand bank of the Nerl, stands an attractive architectural ensemble which includes the **Church of Sts Boris and Gleb**, the first white stone church in North-Eastern Rus, built in 1152.

Kideksha was Yuri Dolgoruky's country residence, and next to the church stood his chambers, but we do not know what they looked like, for time has destroyed not only the buildings but also the earthen ramparts surrounding them. Kideksha has not as yet been thoroughly studied, and future excavations may bring more information to light.

In 1238 Kideksha was pillaged by the Mongol-Tartars; subsequently a monastery was established here, which continued to exist until 1764. These later buildings and the white stone church form an ensemble which blends well into the surrounding countryside.

The Church of Sts Boris and Gleb was built of white stone as the prince's chapel. It has a large triple apse on the river side; each face is divided vertically into three with each section culminating in *zakomary* gables. The bare walls with narrow loop-hole-like windows give the church the appearance of a fortress. The modest blind arcading barely softens the severity of the church, which indeed, was intended to serve as a military stronghold as well.

The church has not come down to us in its original form. The white stone vaults which collapsed were rebuilt in brick, a four-sided sloping roof replaced the old one, of the eastern section only the lower half is original, the large helmet-shaped cupola was replaced by a disproportionately small onion-shaped one, and some of the old windows were filled in and new ones made. Originally the floor was 80 centimetres lower than the present one. The brick entrance on the west side was added in the 19th century.

Only fragments of the 12th century frescoes have survived inside. One shows two horsemen, assumed to be Boris and Gleb. The female figure in the niche on the northern wall is thought to be Yuri Dolgoruky's wife.

The church's particular significance lies in the fact that it was the starting point for all of the stone architecture of Vladimir and Suzdal.

The **Holy Gates** with their decorative front, standing to the south of the Church of Sts Boris and Gleb, were built in the early 18th century, while the winter brick **Church of St. Stephen** was built in 1780 on the site of the former wooden church, of which it is thought to be a copy in its shape. The church is reminiscent of an ordinary dwelling with a gable roof. The extreme simplicity of this small church seems appropriate next to the austere 12th century church, and together they are an example of the happy combination of buildings separated in time by several centuries.

Kideksha: on the left, the bell-tower (18th century); in the centre, the Church of Sts. Boris and Gleb (12th century); and on the right, the Church of St. Stephen (18th century).

The octagonal **bell-tower** on its square base, dating from the 18th century, is similar to many we have already seen in Suzdal, but it lacks their elegance, and is rather more archaic, with its straight-sided rather than concave tent roof. For a long time now it has leant to one side, rather like the Tower of Pisa. The brick wall around the ensemble was rebuilt in 1955.

Kideksha represents the most ancient of all the monuments of Vladimir and Suzdal, and concludes our journey into Russian history. As you stand on the banks of the quiet Nerl, 12th century stones beneath your feet, cast your mind back over the architecture you have seen, for it is a tribute to the ability of man throughout the ages to create things of beauty.

PRACTICAL
INFORMATION

In a souvenir shop

This section provides practical information which may be of use during your stay in Vladimir and Suzdal.

Vladimir is situated 190 kilometres to the east of Moscow, and can be reached by train from Moscow's Kursk Station (the journey takes just over three hours) or by Intourist coach or car.

LOCAL TRANSPORT

Local transport includes trolleybuses, buses and taxis. The fare is four kopecks on trolleybuses and five kopecks on buses, while taxis charge 20 kopecks for every kilometre plus 20 kopecks initial fare. Most trolleybuses and buses operate without conductors.

The No. 103 bus, which leaves from the Park of Vladimir's 850 Anniversary, takes you to Bogolyubovo, 10 kilometres from Vladimir, and from there it is a mere 1.5 kilometres on foot to the Church of the Protecting Veil on the River Nerl.

Buses to Suzdal leave every 30 minutes from the bus station on Vokzalnaya Ploshchad. The distance is 35 kilometres.

Petrol-filling stations are to be found at the entrance to Vladimir both on the Moscow and Gorky roads, and also on the main road into Suzdal.

HOTELS

Vladimir: *Vladimir*–74, ulitsa Tretiego Internatsionala, tel: 30-42
Klyazma–15, Sudogodskoye Shosse, tel: 42-37
Suzdal: The main tourist centre with a hotel for 400, motel for 300, a restaurant catering for 500, cinema cum concert hall, sauna, swimming pool, and bars; tel: 2-15-30

RESTAURANTS

Vladimir: *Vladimir*–at the Vladimir Hotel
The Nerl–61, ulitsa Tretiego Internatsionala

U Zolotykh vorot (At the Golden Gates)–17, ulitsa Tretiego Internatsionala

Traktir (Inn)–2, ulitsa Stolyarova

Suzdal: *Trapeznaya* (Refectory), the restaurant of the main tourist centre, in the Archbishop's Chambers

Gostiny Dvor (Arcade)–Torgovaya Ploshchad

Pogrebok (Wine-Cellar)–6, ulitsa Kremlyovskaya

EXHIBITIONS

Vladimir

History Exhibition–64, ulitsa Tretiego Internatsionala

Military History Exhibition and the Gallery of the Heroes of the Soviet Union–in the Golden Gates (Zolotyie Vorota)

Old Vladimir–in the former water tower on Kozlov Val

Vladimir in Soviet Times–19, ulitsa Mira

Industrial Exhibition–47, Oktyabrsky Prospekt

Exhibition of cut-glass, lacquered miniature and embroidery–in the former Church of the Trinity (Troitskaya) next to the Golden Gates

Exhibition Hall–Park of Vladimir's 850th Anniversary

Temporary exhibitions of painting, drawing and applied art are also held in the Park of Vladimir's 850th Anniversary

The Stoletov Museum–3, ulitsa Stoletovykh

Exhibitions and museums are open from 11 a.m. to 6 p.m. and to 5 p.m. on Tuesdays; the Golden Gates from 10 a.m. to 5 p.m., and to 4 p.m. on Tuesdays. All exhibitions and museums closed on Mondays.

Suzdal

The Leninist Policy of Preserving Historical and Cultural Monuments

Suzdal's History

Old Russian Painting   } The kremlin

The Krestovaya (Cross) Chamber

The Museum of Wooden Architecture and Peasant Life—near the kremlin
The House in the *Posad*—148, ulitsa Lenina

The Office Building
The Linen Industry in Suzdal
The Nuns' Cells
Wood Painting

} The Convent of the Protecting Veil (Pokrovsky Monastyr)

Museum of Amateur Art of the Peoples of the RSFSR
Applied Art of the 13th to 20th Centuries
The Monastery Prison
Exhibition of Books from Six Centuries

} The Monastery of Our Saviour and St. Euthimius (Spasso-Evfimiev Monastyr)

Exhibitions and museums are open from 10 a.m. to 5 p.m., and to 4 p.m. on Mondays. Closed on Tuesdays.

Tripods and flashes must not be used in museums.

ENTERTAINMENT

Drama Theatre—4, ulitsa Moskovskaya
Puppet Theatre—7, ulitsa Gagarina
Taneyev Concert Hall—7, Prospekt Lenina

Cinemas
Khudozhestvenny—13, ulitsa Tretiego Internatsionala
Mir—19, ulitsa Frunze
Burevestnik—29, Prospekt Lenina
Fakel—20, Prospekt Stroitelei
Rus—8, Suzdalsky Prospekt

The Russian Winter Festival is held at the Suzdal tourist centre from the 25th of December to the 5th of January. It includes various fairy-tale characters, a Christmas tree, round dances, singing, clowns, music-hall, troika rides, and other traditional Russian entertainments.

SHOPS

Vladimir
General supermarket—10a, ulitsa Moskovskaya
Lyudmila (goods for women)—19, Prospekt Lenina
Ruslan (goods for men)—20, Prospekt Lenina
Gift Shop—77, ulitsa Gorkogo
Cut-Glass—4, ulitsa Gagarina
Souvenirs—4, ulitsa Gagarina
Local folk art can be bought in the Torgoviye ryady (Shopping arcade)
Suzdal
Suzdalskaya lavka (souvenir shop)—in the kremlin
Torgoviye ryady—the shops here include the *Beriozka* shop, which accepts foreign currency.

Currency exchange. Money can be changed at the state bank in Vladimir at 29, ulitsa Tretiego Internatsionala, open from 9 a.m. to 12.30 p.m., and in the exchange bureau at the tourist centre in Suzdal from 9 a.m. to 18 p.m.

The Main Post-Office—2, ulitsa Podbelskogo, Vladimir

Duty Chemist—3, ulitsa Krasnogo Profinterna, Vladimir

Intourist Office—74, ulitsa Tretiego Internatsionala, Vladimir; tel: 9-75-14

Request to Readers

Raduga Publishers would be glad to have your opinion of this book, its translation and design and any suggestions you may have for future publications.

Please send all your comments to 17, Zubovsky Boulevard, Moscow, USSR.

ИБ № 864

Редактор русского текста М. М. Державина

Контрольный редактор Ю. В. Семенов

Художник Э. М. Симанович

Художественный редактор Н. Н. Щербакова

Технический редактор М. А. Полуян, С. Ф. Сизова

Сдано в набор 20. 09. 82. Подписано в печать 28. 03. 83.
Формат 84 ×108/32. Бумага мелованная. Гарнитура Универс.
Печать офсетная. Условн. печ. л. 7,56.
Уч.-изд. 8,80. Тираж 15670 экз. Заказ № 005351/1.
Цена 1 р. 70 к. Изд. № 35887.

Издательство ,,Радуга'' Государственного комитета
СССР по делам издательств, полиграфии и книжной торговли.
Москва, 119021, Зубовский бульвар, 17

Изготовлено в ГДР.

SUZDAL

KAMENKA

ULITSA LENINA

ULITSA VASILYEVSKAYA

9

1

7

10

10